The Way Women Write

MARY HIATT

Teachers College Press
TEACHERS COLLEGE, COLUMBIA UNIVERSITY
NEW YORK, N.Y. 10027

For
Norman

Copyright © 1977 by
Teachers College, Columbia University.
All rights reserved. Published by Teachers College Press,
1234 Amsterdam Avenue, New York, N.Y. 10027

Library of Congress Cataloging in Publication Data

Hiatt, Mary P   1920–
  The way women write.

  Bibliography: p.
  1. English language–Style   2. English language–
Sex differences. I. Title.
PE1421.H48   810′.9′.9287   77-14122
ISBN 0-8077-2542-0

Manufactured in the United States of America

Contents

List of Tables

Acknowledgments

My efforts to discover whether women and men write differently began in 1973. From that time on, many people have encouraged and supported these efforts in a variety of ways. To all, I offer my deepest gratitude.

In particular, however, I should like to thank Norman Storer, unofficial editor and statistician, Devil's Advocate, and husband; Janet Simons, official editor and friend; and Ray Rauth, kindly computer wizard.

The study was assisted by a Summer Stipend from the National Endowment for the Humanities as well as by the Scholar Assistance Program of Baruch College.

MPH

New York
June 1977

Chapter 1

"The Feminine Style"?

Prologue

In the beginning were man's and woman's words. Man wrote his words; woman did not, being concerned largely with either tempting man or nurturing him and "his" children. Man found another man to write *about* his written words. There were no written words of woman to write about.

And so were created the male writer and the male critic, and they did fruitfully multiply, with a little help from "their" women.

Sometime later, however, woman decided that, in between tempting and nurturing, she could write her words too. And so she began to write.

But the female writer did not fruitfully multiply; she only modestly multipled. And, since there was already an ample supply of male critics quite accustomed to writing about man's writing, who would cheerfully write also about woman's writing, the female critic did not become created, much less multiplied.

The male writers and the male critics, knowing full well that their minds, abilities, and experiences—their very souls, in fact—were infinitely vaster than those of the female writers, thundered, frowned, laughed, or dozed, occasionally all at the same time, at the foolish temerity of the female writers. Dismayed, particularly by the males' laughing and dozing, the female writers sometimes disguised themselves as male writers, but the disguises had a way of becoming revealed.

1

And the thundering, etc., would once again assail the female writers. Nonetheless, they did not disappear; they kept on writing, sometimes secretly and often apologetically. They even found a few women who liked to write about writing.

Faced with this "other" breed of writers and critics, the male writers and critics agreed that, because they themselves were so numerous and were, after all, first on the scene, their writing was of course superior, which is the same as "masculine." The writing of the temerarious women was, logically, inferior, which is the same as "feminine."

Thus it was in the beginning. Thus it has been. Is it still thus?

* * *

Majority-held beliefs, even when found to be untrue, die hard deaths. The belief in a "masculine" versus a "feminine" style has long pervaded literary criticism. The belief, however, has largely gone unchallenged and persists today. It is time for that belief to be questioned, perhaps only because it is so commonly accepted. Even Buffon's famous dictum, "le style est l'homme même," tacitly assumes "la femme même" as separate. But perhaps "le style est la personne même."

The belief in a difference between the ways men and women write may, however, be supported by fact. If so, though, there remain certain other assumptions to be tested. If there exist a masculine style and a feminine style, in what ways are they distinct? How do they differ? Do women write less well than men? Is their style, in other words, "inferior" to that of men? And how is a judgment to be made? Is it even defensible to discuss the style of any *group* of writers, despite the fact that such has been a long-established practice? And, ultimately, if a group does exhitit a style, how do women as a group write?

There is little doubt that male critics of the past and present, without questioning the presumed dichotomy between men's and women's writing styles, have generally considered a "feminine" style inferior. The constant identification of a woman writer *as* a woman writer implies this. She may be "praised" as the "best woman writer alive." Nowhere do we see a male author referred to as the best "man" writer. He is praised as simply the "best writer." Fraya Katz-Stoker maintains that "[the critics] not only emphasize male works, they determine the reasons why the male authors' works are invariably better. This biased criticism is usually conducted under the auspices of formalism (the writing is sentimental, sloppy; the tone is hysterical), but it always results in a nasty attack on women."[1] Southey tells Charlotte Brontë, for example, that literature is not woman's business.[2] As for Emily Brontë, Carol Ohmann has shown us that criticism of *Wuthering Heights* shifts sharply when it becomes known that "Ellis Bell" was a woman. As long as Ellis Bell was assumed to be a man, the language of the novel was compared to that of a "Yorkshire farmer" or "a frequenter of barrooms and steamboat saloons." When the author's identity was revealed, a review comments that the author is a "piteous bird, with wings too weak to fly."[3] James Lane Allen, writing in 1897, declares that "the Feminine Principle" in American fiction consists of "Refinement, Delicacy, Grace, Smallness, Rarity and Tact"—whereas the "Masculine Principle" consists of "Virility, Strength, Massiveness, Largeness, Obviousness, and Primary or Instinctive Action."[4] Leslie Stephen of the Bloomsbury Group uses "masculine" and "manly" to indicate the highest praise and considers "effeminate" and "morbid" synonymous.[5] Walter Pater maintains that "manliness in art" is superior to what is feminine.[6] Jespersen fears that women's expressions will cause language to be "languid and insipid."[7] Hawthorne refers irritably to the "damned scribbling women."[8]

Many contemporary male writers and critics have indulged in similar opinions. Jacques Barzun, in a critique of mystery novels, suggests that the typical aspects of women's lives are concerned with "household confusion," thus generating a "characteristic tone, which one finds faithfully rendered in the 'feminine' detective tale"—reduced to the formula "HIBK" or "Had I But Known."[9] In general, Barzun finds women's mystery novels "passively feminine and feebly spine-chilling."[10] Norman Mailer likens Herbert Gold to a woman writer, obviously the worst comparison that can be made.[11] Leslie Fiedler refers to "lady purveyors of genteel, sentimental fiction" and "scribbling ladies,"[12] but Louis Auchincloss sees other qualities in the writing of women; he states that it is hard for a woman writer to "avoid the strident tone, the shrill cry."[13] David Bromwich comments on Penelope Mortimer's writing in the following manner: "She has the draw-backs of a lyrically fluent 'femininity.' The quotation marks are neces-sary: this is indeed the hothouse or femid [*sic*] sensibility."[14] Sandra Hochman's novel, *Happiness Is Too Much Trouble,* is praised for being "expressed in . . . muscular, masculine prose."[15] Auberon Waugh, in commenting on transsexual Jan Morris' *Travels,* finds that "she now writes in a fine, robust, self-confident style. . . . I should say the new Morris [although now a woman] was noticeably the more mascu-line."[16] Anthony Burgess, reaching into the past, but doubtless ex-pressing implications for the present, complains that Jane Austen's writing "lacks a strong male thrust."[17] Anatomy may or may not be destiny to Burgess, but it certainly seems to be style. This view is also implicit in the rather astounding perorations of William Gass, who finds that "until women can find an openly lustful, quick, impatient, feral hunger in themselves, they will never be liberated, and their writ-ing . . . in pallid imitation of the master, will lack that blood congested genital drive which energizes every great style . . ."[18]

As for female writers and critics, both past and present, they under-standably have followed and are following several paths. Some con-sciously or unconsciously accept the notion that women are inferior writers and thus regard a "feminine" style pejoratively. Others defend a "feminine" style and encourage its development. Both are not unex-pected reactions of any minority faced with an adverse majority.

Jane Austen, for example, seems to agree with Anthony Burgess' evaluation of her own work, for she envies a male writer's "strong, manly spirited sketches, full of variety and glow."[19] George Eliot adopts more than a male name; she adopts male opinion when she refers with scorn to "Silly Novels by Lady Novelists."[20] More recently, Patri-cia Meyer Spacks, in discussing the recognition of female authorship as evidence of the "female imagination," nonetheless castigates Virginia Woolf's "dithery, belle-lettrist style,"[21] presumably a function of Woolf's female imagination. And Mary McCarthy flatly states, "I will not write like a woman."[22]

Other women writers, also agreeing that there is a "feminine" style, regard it with admiration and support and occasionally attempt to de-fine it. Woolf, for example, finds that Dorothy Richardson has developed a "new sentence," a "feminine sentence," a finding that critic Mary Ellmann disputes because the so-called feminine sentence discovered by Woolf also occurs frequently in the writing of men.[23] Annie Gottlieb, in reviewing a book by Tess Slesinger, comments that "There are qualities about Tess Slesinger that are immutably female; and it is a mark of progress that this may now be regarded, not as a handicap but as a definite advantage."[24]

Most of the women writers and critics, however, do not deal with description or definition of a possible "feminine" style so much as they defend against its pejorative connotation. Thus Carolyn Heilbrun, although recognizing that "our definitions of the terms 'masculine' and 'feminine' are little more than received ideas," goes on to say that "masculine" means forceful, vigorous, controlling, competent, etc., and "feminine" means tender, genteel, and sentimental,[25] in themselves not necessarily pejorative adjectives but distinctly so in the eyes of men. Other women critics, such as Ellmann, Rosen, Millett, and Beer,[26] point out that what is perceived by male critics as "feminine" is often expanded or exemplified by such terms as "hysterical," "shrill," "emotional," "silly," "vapid," "oblique," etc.

Women critics further object to the fact that women writers are often caught in the middle of a barrrage of hostile male criticism. A woman's style, for instance, may be considered "feminine," and therefore characterized by a string of the more usual put-down adjectives. Should, however, a woman be considered to write in a "masculine" style, a male critic will either consider that descriptor sufficient praise *or* will, because a woman writing in the "masculine" style is both unseemly and inappropriate and deserves to have this subtly pointed out to her, continue to describe the style as "calculating," "cold," "clinical," and "formidable." Such a woman writer may even be accused of "wielding a riding crop," as has been said of Susan Sontag.[27] We are in this way presented with the unmistakable image of a cruel, punishing woman, and we are supposed to think that her writing style is therefore also cruel and punishing. Mary Ellmann comments that "the fear of similarity rather than of emulation may account for the particularly fierce dislike which men express for primarily decisive women writers like Beauvoir."[28]

Automatic hostile and biased opinion must of course not be countenanced. Ultimately, though, it is the stereotyping of style—or styles—to which women critics object most vehemently. The no-win situation of being branded as silly, incompetent writers ("feminine") or as cold, unfeeling writers ("masculine") is indeed a frustrating one. Josephine Donovan suggests that "close stylistic analyses . . . on an extensive number of women writers would lead us to make further conclusions about 'feminine style.' . . . Surely such an approach is worth further exploration."[29]

A point that critics, both male and female, seem to miss, however, is that impressionistic adjectives do not constitute sound literary criticism. To proclaim that Hemingway's style is "virile" is no more justifiable than labeling Virginia Woolf's style "dithery." Neither adjective has any real meaning. Nonetheless, the impressionistic descriptors march on—"muscular," "manly," "clear," "lush," "lean," "flowery," "sensitive," "exclamatory," "clinical," and so on. Often, too, the adjectives seem to be attached more to the critic's concern with or notions about the gender of an author than with any true stylistic description. We can be fairly certain, for example, that the following adjectives from in a recent review describe a man's writing: "flawless," "plain," "effortless," "terse," and "unsentimental." We can be fairly certain, because these are the ostensible attributes of a man—never of a woman.[30] Karl Kroeber forthrightly declares that "very little of our criticism is honestly exploratory," and that whereas scientists admit failures, "apparently nothing in literary criticism ever fails."[31] He further states that "intuitive evaluations are not 'wrong'—they are just not helpful. They are private. They sum up a complex of personal experience."[32] It may indeed be that intuitive (i.e., impressionistic) evaluations are not wrong, but Kroeber does not elucidate the matter of how they may be *right*. Rightness or wrongness of such evaluations can only depend on solid, objective data and specific definition of terms.

A "lush" style, for example, can only be lush if we know what the critic means by the word and if there is any supporting evidence for its use. Does "lush" mean that the writer employs many liquid sounds? Does it mean that the writer uses many adjectives? Does it mean that the writer favors deeply embedded syntactic structures? Or does it mean none of these? All too often, the specifics are missing. A critic, when asked to define such a term as "lush," will fall back on a string of somewhat synonymous adjectives which themselves require definition. And the metalanguage of style becomes circular.

The reason for the circularity of stylistic description is that what is being described is reader or critic *reaction to* how-something-is-written, rather than how-something-is-written. To describe a house, a car, a boat, a desk as "large," "impressive," "beautiful," or "sleek" is vague, to say the least, and we want to know specifics about size, color, and structure. Even classified advertisements for apartments offer details; few would be interested in an apartment described only as "elegant" or "warm" or "flawless." But in stylistic criticism, such impressionistic generalities are pervasive, because few critics recognize that style itself must be dealt with in discrete elements. A reaction does not a description make, and any adequate description must comprise description of observable, objective aspects of what is being described.

Leaving for a time the questionable practice of assigning convenient adjectives to any individual writer's style, we come to the question of whether there is justification for what might be called "group" labels—such as "masculine" and "feminine." There are stylisticians who hold that style is totally a matter of one individual's writing—that, in effect, there is no such thing as a group style.[33] This seems to be a rather narrow view, given the evidence of shared stylistic and linguistic characteristics of, for instance, the "Attic," the "Baroque," and the "Ciceronian" writers.

Moreover, it seems logical and theoretically entirely defensible to posit that an individual's style can only be claimed individual as it varies from a group style. In other words, a particular writer's style may share many characteristics with that of other writers of his or her linguistic era and may be thought unique only because it has not been compared to a general writing style. In any event, the existence of group styles lies in the objectively discovered occurrence of common traits exhibited by distinct groups, and the individual writer's style can best be evaluated in the context of a particular group style.

If, therefore, contemporary male writers differ stylistically from contemporary female writers, there do exist a masculine style and a feminine style as evidenced by two distinct synchronic groups. But, as discussed previously, this is a matter to be determined, not a matter to be assumed. Before there can be any defense against or accurate appraisal of what Ellmann titles "Phallic Criticism,"[34] i.e., the pejorative masculine views of the writing of women, we must first know whether men and women do indeed write differently and, if so, in what ways. Annette Kolodny supports this stance: "Before we ask *how* women's writing is different or unique, we must first ask *is it?*"[35] Kolodny recommends "rigorous methods for analyzing style and image, and then without preconception or preconceived conclusions . . . apply these methodologies to individual works."[36]

There are studies indicating that the way men and women *speak* does differ. Robin Lakoff, for example, feels that women use more adjectives of admiration than do men and that they tend to use many more tag questions.[37] Her study is not entirely convincing, however, because of an ill-defined and inadequate sample, based on data "gathered mainly by introspection," consisting of her own speech and that of her acquaintances and using her "own intuitions in analyzing it."[38] Mary Ritchie Key's *Male/Female Language* furnishes a very general overview of sexist assumptions about women's roles as reflected in many languages, but offers little in the way of new or useful information.[39] In *Language and Sex,* Barrie Thorne and Nancy Henley offer a limited collection of articles (under the rubric of "sociolinguistics") on speech and language differences between females and males.[40] Of greater value is the work of Cheris Kramer, who, in one paper, reviews much of the research on sex-linked linguistic signals in the United States,[41] and in another, finds that certain *assumptions* about women's speech are not reflected in their writing.[42] Her study of -*ly* adverbs refutes the opinions of Jespersen in that she finds no differences in this usage in the descriptive writing of her students.[43] And sociologist Diana Warshay notes, in her study of sex differences in the writing styles of college students, that women are more fluent than men; they tend to write more and of more events than do the men in her study.[44]

To date, however, there has been no objective study of the possible differences in the writing style of published men and women authors. Such a study is the first order of business and must precede any evaluation of the current critical modes.

For an objective statement concerning the style of a large number of certain writers (e.g., women) compared with the style of a large number of other writers (e.g., men), the services of a computer are necessary. The human critic cannot accurately handle massive amounts of text, for the mind tires and the eye skips. The computer, on the other hand, never forgets.

Unfortunately, to many people, including almost all literary critics, the computer looms as some sort of clinical, impersonal monster. The very word "computer" makes many humanists excessively nervous.

This reaction is derived from what William Nichols perceives as the "modern science-and-humanities debate."[45] The debate is, of course, not new. Nichols cites the exchange between Thomas Carlyle and Timothy Walker in the nineteenth century, in which Carlyle takes the position that "science and technology have brought us something considerably less promising than unalloyed human progress," and might "severely limit our intellectual, emotional and spiritual life," whereas Walker claims that "increasingly complex advances in science and technology offer mankind's primary hope for the future."[46] The debate has more recently been exemplified by the Snow-Leavis controversy, where C. P. Snow is troubled by the lack of contact and the mutual mistrust between the "scientific" and the "humanistic" communities. Nichols, although viewing our ambivalence concerning intricate technical systems as probably healthy, nonetheless warns against surrendering to a "dark Byronic vision of ourselves as cut off by the power of science and technology from all that influences the quality of our external world."[47] Such a "dark Byronic vision" creates the needlessly defensive reactions of the Carlyle-Leavis "axis," in two, equally misguided ways: (1) "I don't know anything about computers, but they are taking over the world and I won't have anything to do with them," and (2) "I don't know anything about computers, but after all, they're only push-button gadgets that can't produce anything worthwhile except bills and bank statements, which they often get wrong."

Both misconceptions are of course founded on ignorance. Not too many people know that there are several computer languages that use English words and accept "data" consisting of real English text. But once that is known, some of the suspicion concerning the computer dissipates. What is a possibly unfathomable and frightening world of numbers and symbols has been replaced by a reassuring world of words.

Furthermore, the computer is a highly complicated and reliable instrument, but one that provides worthwhile answers only insofar as the questions posed are worthwhile. The real power behind the computer throne is the human brain, for the computer does not "do all the work"; it only answers specific questions.

Finding the right questions, however, constitutes considerable work, in this case questions concerning various aspects of style. But if the questions are meaningful in terms of style, and if they are asked correctly—i.e., without programing errors—the computer always gives the correct answers. By contrast, the answers that human beings give are often fallible and subjective or without real meaning. The computer does not "say" that a particular writer or group of writers employs a "hothouse" style, although a human being may find it easy to make such an ill-defined and careless statement.

The right questions concerning style, therefore, should not encompass impressions or intuitions. The right questions are those having to do with such objectively observable matters of style as sentence length, sentence complexity, parallel constructions, rhetorical devices, similes, adjectives, and adverbs. Some of these matters are structural; some are lexical. The computer, however, can also examine logical processes of thought, provided that they are indicated by formal words or phrases. It might be that each area of investigation is clearly delineated, but each area often leads to others, for the computer is a serendipitous instrument and does not simply offer a mass of statistics unless that is all it is asked to do.

But although the computer may offer unexpected "answers" to an inquirer's questions, it in no way takes charge of the study, rendering the investigator a mere slavey. On the contrary, the computer is the slave of the investigator and can unerringly serve an investigator who may be curious as to whether men and women write differently and, if so, in what ways. The computer, in other words, can offer us reliable information as to whether there is a "feminine" style as distinct from a "masculine" style.

Chapter 2

Choosing the Books and Using the Computer

It is obvious that *all* contemporary prose written in English cannot be used as a basis for stylistic evaluation; the astronomical number of words involved would exceed the capabilities of any human researcher even with the extensive aid of a computer. *All* contemporary prose would also not offer an accurate picture of men's and women's writing because *most* contemporary prose is written by men. A reasonably large sampling, however, is needed for a wide-ranging investigation to be cogent.

Accordingly, 100 books were objectively chosen (i.e., not based on the researcher's personal preferences), 50 written by men and 50 written by women.[1] Most critical comment about style is concerned with fiction; therefore half the books are works of fiction. But because non-fiction perhaps constitutes a more stable indicator of style, in that content does not exert as great an influence on style as does fiction content, the other half consists of non-fiction works. The basis for the study, therefore, consists of 25 fiction and 25 non-fiction works by men; and 25 fiction and 25 non-fiction works by women. The books were not randomly chosen in the strictest sense of the word, for certain categories of prose, such as cookbooks and "how-to" books ("How to Build a Boat," "How to Prepare Your Income Tax," etc.), have no stylistic value and yet are printed in large numbers. These categories were therefore excluded. Also excluded was drama, because it is the representation of

11

speech. But beyond these exclusions, the books were chosen simply by plucking them from a bookstore shelf and ascertaining the date of publication. When a particular category became filled, e.g., women's non-fiction, further books in that category were rejected.

Included in the fiction category are Gothic novels (by women) and "adventure" novels (by men), each of which genre may be considered to have its own stylistic properties and thus merely offering "style" appropriate to genre rather than gender. But since the Gothic novel is typically written by women, it can be said to demonstrate evidence of a "feminine" style, and since the "adventure" or "Western" novel is typically written by men, it can likewise consist of a sample of "masculine" style.

The genre-gender question is less prominent in non-fiction, a reason for believing that non-fiction is more truly representative of the differences, if any, between men's and women's writing styles. It is true that few women write of politics, war, and science, but both men and women write biographies and autobiographies, both write critical works, and both write about sex. One could, of course, posit a "biographical" or "autobiographical" style. Nonetheless, it is entirely possible that the way a woman writes a biography is different from the way a man writes one.

Actually, what permeates any discussion of stylistic differences among various genres is the influence of content on style. The influence is undeniable; the language and sentence structure, for example, will vary widely among Gothic novels, mystery novels, childhood memoirs, and film criticism. "Influence" of any sort, however, is very difficult to document, whether of content on style or of one author's writing on that of another. And certainly for a study of style—of any sort—a dualistic approach is necessary. Content and style must be kept separate, although they together form a unitary "work." But if style and content are considered so interwoven as to be indistinguishable—the so-called monistic view derived from Plato via Benedetto Croce—then style ceases to exist at all. And we all know that style does exist, that there are different ways of saying the same thing. Paraphrase alone is ample evidence of this fact. Therefore, although there may be generic differences in style, the over-riding question is still whether a group of women writes in a discernibly different way from a group of men.

The books chosen are all paperbacks, readily available in bookstores. To have selected only hard-cover books would have skewed the sample by limiting it to possibly less representative authors. Paperbacks, on the other hand, have often survived an initial hard-cover printing or have been judged to have an initially wide readership. The "succes d'estime" does not appear in paperback; its author is thus not often a part of the general mass of writers.

This brings up the matter of literary merit. Any study of the writing styles of "recognized" authors cannot be objective, for it would include only those authors selected by the researcher-as-critic as "recognized." In other words, critical opinion would be called into play *before* an assessment of the works, rather than after, and would depend on the subjective critical judgment of the researcher. What is one person's "merit" may well be another person's "trash." Therefore no attempt was made to select only "good" books. Any differences in style between male writers and female writers pervade all their writing, both good and bad. A list of the authors and titles in each category follows in Table 1; full bibliographical information appears in the Appendix.

Among the authors are several who are English: DuMaurier, Mitford, Newman, Rhys, and Burgess. There are others who are probably English, although not so identified in any available information about the author. All of their books, however, are first published in paperback in the United States—i.e., for an American audience. Although there is considerable linguistic difference between spoken British English and spoken American English, there is very little difference evident in their books. Such differences as orthography ("favour" instead of "favor") and occasional verb usage ("I shan't . . ." instead of "I won't . . .") are not matters of style, nor are minor differences in vocabulary ("lift" instead of "elevator"). There was, therefore, no valid reason to reject those novels by English writers on the basis of stylistic variation from the American writers.

As mentioned earlier, all the novels were first published in the late 1960's or early 1970's—with one exception. John O'Hara's book was first published in 1938 but recently reprinted in paperback. It is highly doubtful that the earlier publication date falls in a different linguistic era, and O'Hara's novel therefore is also included in the study.

Table 1. Titles Used In The Study

Fiction Titles

Women	Men
Joan Aiken, *The Fortune Hunters*	Hollis Alpert, *The Summer Lovers*
Martha Albrand, *Wait for the Dawn*	Elliott Arnold, *Walk with the Devil*
Jean Block, *Telfair's Daughter*	Mike Breen, *Zachary*
Alice Boyd, *Two People*	Carter Brown, *The Jade-Eyed Jungle*
Marie Buchanan, *Anima*	Anthony Burgess, *One Hand Clapping*
Joan Didion, *Play It As It Lays*	
Rosalyn Drexler, *To Smithereens*	Lewis Carlino, *The Mechanic*
Daphne DuMaurier, *The Glass Blowers*	Edwin Gilbert, *Newport*
Ann Fairbairn, *Five Smooth Stones*	William Hegner, *The Drum Beaters*
Lois Gould, *Necessary Objects*	George Higgins, *The Friends of Eddie Coyle*
Shirley Ann Grau, *The Black Prince*	James Houston, *The White Dawn*
Victoria Holt, *On the Night of the Seventh Moon*	Elia Kazan, *The Assassins*
Rona Jaffe, *The Other Woman*	Harry Kemelman, *Saturday the Rabbi Went Hungry*
Ruth MacDougall, *The Cheerleader*	Jim Levey, *Partings*
Norma Meacock, *Thinking Girl*	Stephen Longstreet, *The Pedlock Inheritance*
Nancy Mitford, *Pigeon Pie*	
Andrea Newman, *The City Lover*	Ross Macdonald, *Sleeping Beauty*
Joyce Carol Oates, *Them*	Bernard Malamud, *Rembrandt's Hat*
Mary Renault, *The Persian Boy*	

Jean Rhys, *Good Morning, Midnight*
Jeannie Sakol, *I Was Never the Princess*
Alix Kates Shulman, *Memoirs of an Ex-Prom Queen*
Jean Stubbs, *Dear Laura*
Ann Thompson, *A Cry for Love*
Dorothy Uhnak, *Law and Order*

John O'Hara, *Hope of Heaven*
Philip Roth, *The Great American Novel*
Wilfred Sheed, *People Will Always Be Kind*
Charles Simmons, *An Old-Fashioned Darling*
Wilbur Smith, *Gold Mine*
Fred Stewart, *Lady Darlington*
Kurt Vonnegut, *Slaughterhouse Five*
Irving Wallace, *The Seven Minutes*
Tom Wicker, *Facing the Lions*

Non-Fiction Titles

Women

Joyce Brothers, *The Brothers System for Liberated Love and Marriage*
Barbara Cartland, *Josephine: Empress of France*
Phyllis Chesler, *Women and Madness*
Susan Cohen, *Liberated Marriage*
Agnes DeMille, *Speak to Me, Dance with Me*
Frances Farmer, *Will There Really Be a Morning?*
Florence Fisher, *The Search for Anna Fisher*
Frances FitzGerald, *Fire in the Lake*
Nancy Friday, *My Secret Garden*

Men

Carl Belz, *The Story of Rock*
Rudolf Bing, *5000 Nights at the Opera*
Gary Carey, *Brando!*
Frederick Cartwright, *Disease and History*
Ronald Clark, *Einstein: The Life and Times*
Frank Edwards, *Strange People*
Albert Ellis, *The Sensuous Person*
Joseph Goodavage, *The Comet Kohoutek*
Graham Greene, *A Sort of Life*
Walter Langer, *The Mind of Adolf Hitler*
Joseph Lash, *Eleanor and Franklin*
Peter Maas, *Serpico*

Ruth Gordon, *Myself Among Others*

Jane Hodge, *Only a Novel*

Marjorie Holmes, *I've Got to Talk to Somebody, God*

Penelope Houston, *The Contemporary Cinema*

Barbara Howar, *Laughing All the Way*

Eda LeShan, *Sex and Your Teen-Ager*

Anne Lindbergh, *Hour of Gold, Hour of Lead*

Joyce Maynard, *Looking Back*

Kate Millett, *Sexual Politics*

Ruth Montgomery, *Here and Hereafter*

Elaine Morgan, *The Descent of Woman*

Mary Ann Oakley, *Elizabeth Cady Stanton*

Marion Sanders, *Dorothy Thompson*

Flora Schreiber, *Sybil*

Nancy Steiner, *A Closer Look at Ariel*

Esther Vilar, *The Manipulated Man*

Norman Mailer, *Of a Fire on the Moon*

John Mander, *The Unrevolutionary Society*

Frank Mankiewicz, *Perfectly Clear*

Lawrence Peter, *The Peter Prescription*

Oliver Pilat, *Drew Pearson*

George Plimpton, *Hank Aaron: One for the Record*

Norman Rosten, *Marilyn*

Richard Rovere, *The American Establishment*

Harrison Salisbury, *To Peking—And Beyond*

Frank Smith, *The Politics of Conservation*

Telford Taylor, *Nuremburg and Vietnam*

Hunter Thompson, *Fear and Loathing on the Campaign Trail*

Alvin Toffler, *Future Shock*

A few comments are in order concerning the non-fiction sample. Twelve of the books by women can be classified as biography or autobiography; ten of the men's books fall in the same classification. The total sample is thus acceptably balanced in this particular, even though they were not selected to fill any sort of "quota." In other respects, however, the subject matter of the non-fiction is much broader among the men writers than among the women. Six of the women's books, for example, can be classified as concerning sex and/or marriage (Brothers, Cohen, Friday, LeShan, Morgan, and Vilar), whereas only one male book concerns itself with sex (Ellis). Only one woman (FitzGerald) writes of politics and/or political science; seven men's books fall in this category (Mander, Mankiewicz, Rovere, Salisbury, Smith, Taylor, and Thompson). The concerns of the men and the women are obviously vastly different and in general reflect the more limited and personal subject matter of the women.

One book (Vilar) was discovered to be a translation of a work originally published in German. It was initially rejected but ultimately included in the sample because the translation is in completely idiomatic English.

The books chosen form the basis of a synchronic study, that is, one concerned with a specific time. Almost all were published in the United States during the 1960's and 1970's—or within one linguistic era. To have included books written during, say, the Victorian era, would doubtless reveal stylistic differences between Victorian writers and present-day writers—but then one would not know whether gender or history had created the differences. A synchronic, rather than an historical or diachronic, approach eliminates variance due to the general changes in language and style over a span of time.

This is not to say that a wide-ranging study of the possible sex differences in style in the prose of another century would not be of considerable interest. In fact, it is almost certain that any differences between men's and women's writing occurring in, for example, the nineteenth century would be even more marked than in the prose of today, for women's lives were far more circumscribed then than they are now. Differences, in other words, might be progressively disappearing, insofar as they are culturally determined.

The basic sample, therefore, consists of 100 paperbacks published in the late 1960's or early 1970's, with each of the 50-book men's and women's subsamples further equally divided into fiction and non-fiction. In view of the entire "universe" of published prose, this may seem to be a small, rather than a large, sample. But when one considers the number of words involved, it becomes a very large sample indeed. If each book consists of approximately 90,000 words, the 100 books provide nine million words of text—again an unmanageable amount.

From each book, therefore, four 500-word passages were chosen randomly, using a random number table. There are no consecutive passages. In the fiction category, such a method of selection might result in passages comprising dialogue alone, not a very accurate measure of a writer's style. The procedure used by Henry Kučera and Nelson Francis in their million-word sample of present-day prose was therefore followed.[2] Kučera and Francis excluded all passages of fiction that contained more than 50 percent dialogue, on the basis that a passage consisting entirely of dialogue was not representative fiction.

Four 500-word passages from each book constitute 2000 words of running text per book—or 200,000 words in the total study.

It is unfortunate that thus far computers cannot read books. If they could, the passages could be "fed" directly to a computer without any further preparation. But computers, as we know, generally deal with the do-not-fold-spindle-or-mutilate cards. The entire 200,000 words were therefore keypunched onto IBM cards. This is a tedious job, but one that any reasonably competent typist can perform. There is no "magic" involved in the process. The precise words of the 100 authors were keypunched onto the cards without changing the words into numerical codes. The keypunch machine, very similar to a typewriter, not only types the words across the top of the card, but also punches out little holes below, the arrangement of which represents the letters in the words. The only "code" used is the author/passage identification at the end of each card, in the last seven spaces.

Perhaps the most mysterious process of computer use for most of us is the computer "program," involving as it does a computer "language." A program is essentially a sequence of instructions to the computer (also keypunched onto cards) as to what the computer should do with the "data," in this case, the 200,000 words of fiction and non-fiction. A relatively simple program, for example, would be one instructing the computer to scan each of the cards containing the text, to find each instance of the word "like" or "as" in each card, and to print only those sentences containing those words. Thus, because a simile is always indicated by the words "like" and "as," the printed sentences (called, in this case, "print-out") would contain all the similes in the 200,000 words of text. It is obvious, of course, that the two words may *not* introduce a simile, as in "They like to cook," or "Today's weather is as hot as yesterday's." The print-out therefore will also contain such non-simile sentences, but it is easy simply to cross these out. At least one can be sure that the similes are all accounted for, something that is uncertain if one tries to *read* the text for all similes.

Some programs are of course more complicated than the one briefly outlined above, but the major part of any computer program is a search in the data for the presence (or absence) of certain elements, whether they be numbers or words or other types of symbols. Once an "element" is discovered, a program may encompass other instructions, such as counting, deleting, changing the order of elements, replacing with other elements—or simply printing.

Computer "languages" are numerous and acronymic. Most of us have heard of FORTRAN, some of us have heard of COBOL—those are the most generally known and used because of their wide applicability to numerical problems. Both are written in numbers and symbols, and neither can deal with words-as-data. A computer language such as BASIC is written in words, but it also cannot deal with words-as-data. A computer language that does deal with words-as-data is SNO-BOL.[3] This is a "powerful" language in that a program written in it can do many things, but it is not difficult language to learn. It is the chief language used in this study of "masculine" and "feminine" style, although one other, less powerful, system, WYLBUR, is also employed for a program that does not require the complexity of instructions necessary in the other programs.

Anyone studying a large amount of text by means of a computer has the option, however, of *not* learning a computer language and *not* writing any computer programs. There are many persons in the computer field who can perform such work and cooperate in any such study. Most research of this nature, as a matter of fact, is carried out with the aid of a consultant or assistant conversant with the uses of the computer, and the so-called chief investigator is responsible for the areas to be investigated, the general direction of the work, and at least some interpretation of the findings.[4]

But there is a disadvantage in not becoming directly involved with the computer; one may not know whether the findings do in fact reflect "answers" to the "questions" asked, for one is not certain that the questions verbally posed are being "asked" accurately in the computer programs. Something, in other words, may become lost in translation—the translation from the words of the researcher to the programs written by the computer expert. The situation is somewhat analogous to speaking through an interpreter. No matter how efficient or accurate the interpreter is, the speaker who does not understand what is being said feels some loss of contact in the discourse. It is more satisfying to learn the language, for only then is one certain of the answers.

At any rate, in the particular study at hand, the rewards of some knowledge of computer programing more than offset the time spent acquiring the knowledge. The entire study was what is called by computer people a "hands-on" process, with the researcher's direct involvement with the computer. Nine computer programs were written, eight in SNOBOL and one utilizing WYLBUR, concerned with various aspects of style. The findings are compared for each of the two groups—male writers of fiction and non-fiction and female writers of fiction and non-fiction—in the ensuing chapters.

Chapter 3

Longwindedness Versus Shortwindedness

The gossip, the shrew, the nag—standard masculine stereotypes for women—are all depicted as excessive talkers who go on and on. Men, on the other hand, are often portrayed by both men and women as strong, silent types, verbally terse. Terse, pithy utterances are regarded somehow as evidence of masculine strength and unflappability; loquaciousness is regarded as evidence of disorganized and uncontrolled emotions, of compulsiveness.

That these are only stereotypes should be evident to anyone who has heard male academics drone on and on at faculty meetings or who has listened to a man describe in endless detail every stroke (and every thought while making every stroke) of a golf game or who has been the unwilling audience at a male "bull session." Women do gossip; so do men and in at least equal detail. Women sometimes ramble; so do men, at least as often.

But at the heart of the stereotype of the endlessly chattering woman is another unexamined belief—that *what* women say is inconsequential and what *what* men say is important and very consequential. The male utterance, regardless of content, is therefore accorded respect and authority simply because it is uttered by a male.

In the face of considerable evidence that women as a group are more fluent than men—that is, that they acquire and use language more easily than do men—"fluency" is nonetheless a term rarely used in describing women's style; it is too commendatory a term. The pejorative substitutes persist, and the males' comparative lack of fluency is transmuted into admirable terseness.

An examination of one aspect of writing style—sentence length—offers no support for the stereotypes, for in general the women in this study phrase their thoughts in shorter, rather than longer, units than do the men. In written style, the women are more terse than the men.

Non-Fiction

Between the male and female writers of non-fiction, the difference in average sentence length is not significant, with the men's average sentence length only slightly longer than that of the women. The male writers' average is 23 words per sentence; the women writers' average sentence length is 21 words.

The gross averages (23 and 21 words per sentence), however, do not tell the whole story. Nor does range of sentence length, for in terms of range the women and men non-fiction writers are not different. The men's average sentence lengths vary from 15 words per sentence to 33 (an 18-word range); the women's sentences average from 12 words per sentence to 31 (a 19-word range). But a comparison of the very short sentences (under six words) as used by the two groups reveals that the number of women's sentences under six words is almost double the number of those used by men.

Dividing all the sentences into two groups, those of twenty words or fewer ("short," but not just the "very short" sentences) and those of more than twenty words ("long" sentences), is even more revealing. Analysis indicates that women use significantly more short sentences (58 percent of their sample versus 48 percent of the sentences in the men's sample) and thus significantly fewer long sentences. Therefore, despite a difference of only two words in the *average* sentence length of the two groups, a much wider difference is evident at the two ends of the spectrum of sentence length, with the women's predominant at the lower end. The pattern underlying the women's generally shorter sentences can be seen in Table 2.

Women write 1445 sentences of from 1 to 20 words, compared to

Table 2. Frequency Distribution of Sentence Lengths: Non-Fiction Sample

Sentence Length (words)	No. of Instances— Men	No. of Instances— Women
1-5	66	113
6-10	258	379
11-15	364	494
16-20	388	459
21-25	338	308
26-30	296	270
31-35	195	170
36-40	126	115
41-50	123	111
51-60	44	44
61-70	28	22
71-80	12	5
81-90	5	3
91-100	3	0
Over 100	3	0

1076 men's sentences of the same length, or 25 percent more of such sentences. After 20 words, the proportion (with the exception of sentences from 51-60 words) changes, with women writing consistently fewer of the longer sentences. So much for the notion that women ramble on interminably.

Because 22 of the 50 non-fiction works by men and women are either autobiographies or biographies (see Chapter 2), it is worth considering whether genre might affect sentence length. Two male autobiographies, those of Rudolf Bing and Graham Greene, were compared with two women's autobiographies, those of Ruth Gordon and Agnes De-Mille. Both Gordon, whose average sentence length is 13 words, and DeMille, with an average sentence length of 12 words, use far shorter sentences than do their male counterparts. Bing's average sentence is 29 words, and Greene's is 24 words. The two female autobiographies fall far below the average sentence length for women's non-fiction (21 words), whereas the male autobiographies are both above the average sentence length of male non-fiction, 23 words per sentence.

Content, in this instance, would not seem to be the reason for the great differences in sentence length between these male and female writers, for all four autobiographies are concerned with the lives of persons in the world of theater, literature, and music. It might therefore be concluded that the way these women-in-the-arts tell their life stories is simply different from the way the two men-in-the-arts perform the same task. And indeed this is the case.

The two women are concerned with their adventures or misadventures with men or with colleagues. Their autobiographies are studded with personal anecdotes and with dialogue. Sentences in dialogue are almost always shorter than those of other types of prose writing. The aim of both women, apparently, is to please, to be charming, witty, and amusing. This aim can fairly be said to be a manifestation of the type of approval-seeking behavior of which women in general are often accused. They "win" by cajoling, by a subtle sort of seductiveness, by pretending that they aren't serious.

Bing, by contrast, seeks *his* approval by long, detailed accounts of his power in the opera world. He hires and fires and argues and justifies his decisions. He is never wrong. He is deadly serious. His aim is not to amuse, it is to impress. He employs what Ellmann refers to as the "authoritative tone,"[1] and he "wins" by authority, not by seduction.

There is little introspection in the autobiographies of Gordon, De-Mille, and Bing. And in this particular matter, Greene's autobiography is different from the other three, for it is a very introspective account of his career as a writer. It is also a modest account, as demonstrated even by its title: *A Sort of Life.* Greene seems to be seeking no one's approval but his own.

There are only four other autobiographies in the non-fiction category, all by women. Of these, the average sentence lengths of Frances Farmer's and Anne Lindbergh's autobiographies fall below the average sentence length for women's non-fiction, with both women at 17 words per sentence. Barbara Howar's average is 22 words per sentence, and

Joyce Maynard's is considerably above the average at 27 words per sentence. Therefore the *drastically* shorter-than-average sentence lengths of the Gordon and DeMille autobiographies are not typical of the women's autobiographies. But whereas there are more autobiographies by women in the study than by men, it is still true that of the women's autobiographies, four of the six have *relatively* short average sentence lengths.

Although the tone of Howar's *Laughing All the Way* is akin to that of the DeMille and Gordon autobiographies, her method is somewhat different; it is anecdotal, but not studded with dialogue. The tone of the other three women's autobiographies is serious and introspective, in no way frivolous. Their aim is neither to please nor to impress; the quality of their memoirs is closer to that of Graham Greene's.

In view of the fact that there are six autobiographies by women and only two by men, thus consisting of a skewed sample of autobiographies, it is more cogent to examine the combination of biographies and autobiographies by men and women, where the two categories are closer in size, with ten biographies/autobiographies by men and twelve biographies/autobiographies by women. (A precise numerical matching of these types of prose would have undercut the goal of randomness of the selection process.)

Of the ten male writers of biography and autobiography, six (60 percent) manifest an average sentence length shorter than the 23-word average of male non-fiction and 24-word average of the other categories of male non-fiction. Norman Rosten's biography *Marilyn* and Peter Maas' *Serpico,* for example, have average sentence lengths of 15 and 16 words respectively. And, as with the Gordon and DeMille autobiographies, these biographies are highly anecdotal and replete with short-sentence dialogue. Nine (or 75 percent) of the women writers of biography and autobiography, on the other hand, have average sentence lengths shorter than the 21 words that is the average for women's non-fiction and the 22-word average that is the average of the other categories of female non-fiction. The woman's biography with the shortest average sentence length is Mary Ann Oakley's *Elizabeth Cady Stanton* (17 words).

Furthermore, within the entire group of 25 men non-fiction writers, only 14 (or 56 percent) have average sentence lengths falling below 23 words, whereas 16 (or 64 percent) of the 25 women in the women's non-fiction sample have average sentence lengths below 21 words. There does seem, therefore, to be some influence of genre on sentence length, for the biographies and autobiographies of both men and women generally employ shorter sentences. This is probably accounted for by the narrative nature of much of the genre, and by the aforementioned use of dialogue. Even within the genre, however, the men's sentences are longer than the women's.

A consideration of the *longer* sentences of both the men and women writers of non-fiction reveals further differences. The three top "long-sentence-writers" of each group do not differ much in sentence length. Norman Mailer (33 words per sentence), Telford Taylor (31 words), and George Plimpton (30 words—the only "long-sentence-writer" of biography) are almost precisely matched by their female counterparts: Penelope Houston (31 words), Ruth Montgomery (31 words), and Frances FitzGerald (30 words). The differences become apparent only when *all* non-fiction writers whose average sentence lengths are above average for their group are studied.

Generally speaking, the longer the sentence, the more likely it is to be structurally complex. The long sentence will contain clauses, modifiers, inserts, appositives, and conjunctions not found in the short sentence. (Structural complexity, it must be noted, is quite different from lexical complexity. A structurally simple sentence such as "Ontogeny recapitulates phylogeny" is lexically complex.) Therefore, both the men's and the women's long sentences are complex—but in different ways.

Hunter Thompson, for example, has an average sentence length of 24 words, not much above the men's non-fiction average. But in his longer sentences, he uses many dashes—28 altogether in the 2000-word sample from his *Fear and Loathing on the Campaign Trail*—which serve to set off what might be called after-thoughts or self-interrupters:

> *As it turned out, neither Humphrey nor McGovern did anything dramatic when they got back to Washington—or at least anything public—and a week or so later the New York Times announced that. . . .*[2]

> *A convention packed wall to wall with Muskie delegates— the*
> *rancid cream of the party, as it were—would make short work of*
> *McGovern's Boy Scout bullshit.*

The first sentence is a compound sentence with two clauses in the first element and one in the second. The second sentence is actually a simple sentence. But both are rendered much more complex by the phrases inserted between the dashes, which serve to "loosen" the syntactic organization of the sentence.

Plimpton (30-word average; *Hank Aaron: One for the Record)* also uses many dashes (31 in all) and displays the added complexity and looseness of style created by such use:

> *But how strange of this in terms of a baseball game, and the*
> *assurance that their man is going to hit a home run for them—an*
> *impossibly difficult feat—after all how many times did Aaron. . . .*

> *All of those I saw were black—ample cheerful men in the eleva-*
> *tors, always wearing ties, and I was never able to catch their eye*
> *for a morning greeting.*

> *It's a poor area, and the old man—his name is Bailey—sells his*
> *cement blocks for ten dollars—to set flat in the cemetery grass with*
> *the name and the date—what in marble would cost a hundred*
> *dollars.*

The last sentence is actually quite difficult to analyze syntactically simply because of the dashes, although it seems to be a compound sentence with one clause.

Bing's sentences in his autobiography employ many complicated series, all in perfectly parallel constructions, as in

> *All my year was busy with Glyndebourne—engaging the artists,*
> *planning the rehearsals and the season, having the tickets*
> *printed, looking after the catering arrangements, organizing the*
> *box office, fighting with the railroad about the train arrange-*
> *ments, seeing to the bus service from Lewes to the theater, making*

> *sure our artists would have the accommodations they required, on Christie's estate or in Lewes, and so forth.*

Frederick Cartwright (average 24 words; *Disease and History*) uses "right-branching" sentences, that is, sentences with long predications containing most of the information of the sentence. Many of his sentences begin with "It is true that . . ." or "It was evident that . . . ." The use of the pronoun "it" in this manner, i.e., as an "empty" subject at the beginning of the sentence, throws the real subject toward the end of the sentence. Such a pattern produces length and structural complexity, but it tends to make the writing easier to understand, for the reader does not have to "remember" the subject until the sentence is ended. Cartwright rarely begins his sentences with introductory adverbial clauses or phrases, preferring to plunge in with his "it." Subordination thus occurs in the predicate.

Telford Taylor (average 31 words; *Nuremburg and Vietnam*) employs many restrictive clauses in his longer sentences, such as

> *Unless troops are trained and required to draw the distinction between military and nonmilitary killings, and to retain such respect for the value of life that unnecessary death and destruction will continue to repel them, they may lose the sense for that distinction for the rest of their lives.*

> *What has been released is, however, of great interest in that it describes the history and training of the units and headquarters involved at Son My, and mentions and quotes from a number of the tactical and other directives that are supposed to govern the conduct of military operations in Vietnam.*

These sentences are highly complex and tightly organized. The reader cannot afford to miss a word or phrase, something that is easy to do when reading Thompson or Plimpton.

Frank Smith (average 27 words; *The Politics of Conservation*), on the other hand, demonstrates a predilection for apposition, and it is through this particular syntactic device that his longer sentences become complex, for many linguists maintain that an appositive plus what it is in apposition to forms a verbless sentence. Examples of Smith's appositive-prone style follow:

> *Chief among them was Daniel Tompkins, Governor of the State, and about to become the next Vice-President of the United States, in keeping with the tradition of . . . .*

> *John W. Davis, the noted lawyer who was the Democratic nominee for President in 1924, identified the bill . . . .*

> *Wilson's Secretary of the Navy, Josephus Daniels, had jealously guarded the three tracts from attempts by Secretary Lane . . . .*

> *Before long, the President was advising Secretary of Agriculture Wilson, Pinchot's long-time supporter and superior, to try to curb some of the publicity . . . .*

Norman Mailer's sentences (average 33 words; *Of a Fire on the Moon*) are especially complicated and demonstrate lengthy seriation, many parenthetical phrases and clauses, and many phrasal and clausal modifiers. The following sentence, for example, is not only long but difficult to understand because of the complexity of structure:

> *On the one hand to dwell in the very center of technological reality (which is to say that world where every question must have answers and procedures, or technique cannot itself progress) yet to inhabit—if only in one's dream—that other world where death, metaphysics and the unanswerable questions of eternity must reside, was to suggest natures so divided that they could have been the most miserable and unbalanced of men if they did not contain in their contradictions some of the profound and accelerating opposites of the century itself.*

The sentence is not atypical of the overinflated, convoluted, antithetical, and embedded structure of the sentences in the rest of the Mailer sample. A reader might justifiably suspect that Mailer is showing off or trying to demonstrate his verbal virtuosity.

The complexity of the sentence structure of yet another male writer with an average sentence length above the group average for men is a bit less clear to define. Richard Rovere (averge 28 words; *The American Establishment*) often employs seriation, as in

> *Next, a local beauty, a local union man, or a local Kiwanis man hand the President, depending on where we are, a bag of peaches, a mess of celery, a miner's hat, or just the key to the city.*

> *He begins with local scenery, local industry, local agriculture, and local intelligence; leads from this into a description of the contempt in which the Republican Party holds the region he is passing through; goes on to a preview of the Good Society that he, given another term and the kind of Congress he wants, will create; and, penultimately, makes his plea for votes.*

But the seriation is mainly confined to passages describing the campaign techniques of the then-President, Truman. At other times, Rovere employs a wide range of syntactic techniques lending complexity to his sentences: introductory adverbial clauses, parenthetical material, and so forth. In other words, there does not seem to be a particular type of complex sentence that he favors—other than the aforementioned seriation in some circumstances.

The remaining two male writers of longer-than-average sentences, Frank Mankiewicz (average 28 words; *Perfectly Clear*) and Graham Greene (average 24 words; *A Sort of Life*) similarly do not select any one particular pattern of complexity in their long sentences. But of the eleven male writers whose average sentence length is above the average for all male non-fiction writers in the sample, eight of them exhibit specific, often repeated, patterns of style.

Such is not so often the case with the women non-fiction writers. Eda LeShan (average 27 words; *Sex and Your Teen-ager*), for example, uses many dashes also (cf. Hunter Thompson and George Plimpton), but the units of her sentences are shorter and less complicated:

> *If we are open to change, and flexible enough to see some values in new ideas, then as partners with young people, we will be allowed—perhaps even encouraged and asked—to point out those fundamental and eternal verities that do not change, that have validity and meaning—that give hope and purpose and meaning to life—despite change.*

The sentence is undeniably long, but its elements are somewhat repetitive, even redundant. There is not any real interjection of new or stray thoughts as usually signaled by the use of dashes. Rather, LeShan tends, through her dashes, merely to reinforce previous statements by changing the wording a bit.

Joyce Maynard (average 27 words; *Looking Back*) likewise lengthens her sentences by means of dashes. She also employs parentheses, but in her case, many of the constructions set off in such a way could have been separate sentences and only rarely indicate interruption of thought by adding "new" thought:

> *My father always offered to drive to the dance (So did my mother—she would pull up slowly to get a look at all the boys and point out the cute ones, while I sank in the seat and hoped she wouldn't kiss me goodbye).*

> *It was words like "special" and "miracle" and "gift," the notion of woman's secret burden, with connotations of brave, silent suffering (The boys would never know what we went through—for them; we'd let them think they were the tough ones)—that's what I detested, and why I entered adolescence with some amount of anguish.*

Four of the other seven female authors with sentence lengths greater than the average for the women's non-fiction sample (21 words) show great variety in what might be called the stratagems of complexity. That is, the complexity of their longer sentences is occasioned by a variety of syntactic devices. Frances FitzGerald (average 30 words; *Fire in the Lake*), Kate Millett (average 28 words; *Sexual Politics*), Ruth

Montgomery (average 31 words; *Here and Hereafter*), and Elaine Morgan (average 22 words; *The Descent of Woman*) all employ a range of syntactic patterns in their long sentences: introductory adverbial phrases and clauses, clausal and phrasal modifiers, appositives, etc.

The remaining three women non-fiction writers employ seriation in their longer sentences, with Penelope Houston (average 31 words; *The Contemporary Cinema*) using more series and more complicated series than the others:

> *Hitchcock has always been a past-master of the planned incongruity: a crop-dusting aeroplane comes out of a quiet sky to spray bullets at a man standing alone in the stubble; a corpse, impudent and accusing, lies amid the red autumn leaves of a New England wood; a near-strangling ruffles the polite surface of a diplomatic party.*

> *Murder in the United Nations building; at a funfair (with, as an extra refinement, the whole scene reflected in a lens of the victim's spectacles); in a run-down motel; in a New York block of flats, with James Stewart across the courtyard to witness it.*

> *His comic subjects—the sustained transvestist joke of "Some Like It Hot," the post-war Berlin of fraternization and the black market ("A Foreign Affair"), the Berlin crisis ("One, Two, Three"), the amalgam of sex and office politics in "The Apartment"—have generally been exercises, more or less successful, more or less desperate, in seeing what might be done with a bad-taste joke, or how to be vulgar and funny.*

The foregoing are examples of heavily embedded seriation, rather than the more simple types of series used by Barbara Howar (average 22 words; *Laughing All the Way*) and Nancy Friday (average 23 words; *My Secret Garden*). The former lists the activities and items involved in her position with President Johnson's family:

> *Mornings were spent in my inaugural office arranging for ca-*

*terers, meeting with hotel managers, arguing about liquor li-
censes and special seating arrangements for Lyndon's Cousin
Oriole or Hubert's Minneapolis mayor.*

*Afternoons were spent in department stores selecting dozens of ball
gowns, suits, dresses, hats, shoes, gloves, and purses for the Johnson
girls.*

The latter (Friday) uses series in describing the functions or possibilities
of fantasies:

*They expand, heighten, distort or exaggerate reality, taking one
further, faster, in the direction in which the unashamed unconscious already knows it wants to go.*

*They exist only for their elasticity, their ability to instantly in-
corporate any new character, image, or idea—or, as in dreams, to
which they bear so close a relationship, to contain conflicting ideas
simultaneously.*

Neither Howar nor Friday, however, uses seriation throughout her
sample; it is not, therefore, a consistent characteristic of their style (cf.
Rovere).

In summarizing the characteristics of the non-fiction writers of
longer-than-average sentences and hence the nature of their more complex sentences, we find that eight of the eleven male writers exhibit
often repeated patterns specific to the writer. Two do not choose any
particular pattern and their syntactic designs are hence more varied; one
uses a particular pattern in particular contexts. On the other hand, only
three of the nine female writers of longer-than-average sentences consistently repeat particular patterns: Maynard and LeShan (dashes, which
often do not denote interruption of thought and in this sense are not
real indicators of complexity) and Houston (complex series). The other
six show varied patterns of complexity. They favor no single pattern of
style.

It can be claimed, therefore, that fewer of the female non-fiction writers possess a noteworthy style than do their male counterparts. In only three female writers does a particular, individual, and repeated pattern "jump out" at the reader. By the same token, however, it can be claimed that the women non-fiction writers are more flexible stylistically because they *do* employ a wider range and a greater variety of patterns. They are not so fixated on one sentence pattern as are the men.

In general, of course, because the women non-fiction writers write shorter sentences than do the men, their sentences are less complex. But the nature of their stylistic complexity is far less individualized than is that of the men. Perhaps it is just that they do not "dare" as does a Mailer, preferring to set down their thoughts in an orderly and relatively unstrained fashion.

Compared to the men writers of non-fiction, they are short-winded. It is the tendency of the men to go on and on.

Fiction

It is entirely unsurprising that the average sentence lengths for both the men and the women in the fiction sample fall notably below those of the non-fiction sample. Moreover, in the case of fiction, the average sentence length of men's and women's fiction is almost exactly the same: 16.84 words per sentence for the men and 16.44 words for the women. Four-tenths of a word does not a significant difference make.

Dialogue, of course, is chiefly accountable for the shorter sentences in fiction, but, as mentioned earlier, no passage with more than 50 percent dialogue is included in the study. The fiction sample thus does include narrative, descriptive, and some expository prose, as well as passages of interior monologue. The latter might be claimed to constitute a form of "dialogue," as it usually follows the patterns of speech rather than written expression, but because the fiction authors in the sample vary enormously in the extent to which they employ this device, it is simply assigned to the general "non-dialogue" aspect of fiction writing.

If, however, the masculine utterance is typically "terse" and "pithy," the same claim can be made for the feminine utterance in view of the same average sentence lengths for men's and women's fiction. Terseness as a masculine characteristic must be dismissed, because for every verbal exchange by a Lewis John Carlino (average 13 words; *The Mechanic*), as exemplified by the following:

> *"Tomorrow night. Eleven. I'll take you."*
> *"We'll have to use your car. Mine's in the shop. Transmission*
> *trouble."*
> *"Sure."*

there is a Joan Didion (average 15 words; *Play It As It Lays*) counterpart:

> *"I mean the teacher, she. She carries the picture."*
> *"The teacher," Maria said.*

But, as in non-fiction, average sentence lengths do not tell the whole story. The fiction sentences of women differ from those of men in one clear-cut manner: the range of their sentence lengths is notably shorter than that of men. The highest averages for the men fiction writers are 30 and 27 words per sentence; the highest for women is 23 and 22 words per sentence. The lowest for both groups is 13 words per sentence, manifested by three male writers and two female writers. The longest sentence in each of the 25 male fiction writers ranges from 30 words to 116 words; a similar examination of the longest sentence in each woman's fiction shows a range from 31 words to 90 words. There is thus some indication that, although the averages for the two groups are the same, the male writers do write more very long sentences than the women, and also many short sentences.

Of the two male writers with the highest average sentence lengths, Tom Wicker (average 30 words; *Facing the Lions*) and Anthony Burgess (average 27 words; *One Hand Clapping*), their longest sentences are 104 words and 86 words, respectively:

> *For the first time in years Morgan thought of his cousin Liza;*
> *and even in the harsh morning sun, even among the pieces of*
> *plastic furniture and the cheap modern prints and the gaudy thin*
> *carpeting of the Bright Leaf Motel, he could see again in mind's*
> *eye his Aunt Octavia's huge, dim kitchen, the dark corner beyond*

the wood range, the patterned linoleum, the round oaken table on its pedestal in the middle of the floor; he heard the sharp slap of the screen door behind him as he fled the big old gloomy kitchen to the side back porch. (Wicker)

Then there was a bit of a variety show which Howard said was really depressing, though I thought it was rather pretty and funny really, then we had this play and it was the same sort of thing as the copper's nark thing we'd just had, with a husband and wife quarreling like mad and throwing the milk jug and then the husband took a knife to her and she ran away from him screaming and then she fell through the bannister rails which were broken. (Burgess)

Wicker's shortest sentence, however, lest he be accused of going on and on, contains only two words; Burgess' shortest sentence, four. Wicker's range, therefore, is from 2 to 104 words, and Burgess' from 4 to 86 words. Thus the range of the two male fiction writers with the highest average sentence length is 102 and 82 words respectively.

The two women writers of fiction with the highest average sentence lengths are Daphne DuMaurier (average 23 words; *The Glass Blowers*) and Nancy Mitford (average 22 words; *Pigeon Pie*). DuMaurier's longest sentence is 86 words, the same as Burgess':

During that winter of '93, as we read our Ami du Peuple *and learnt of the continuing division within the convention, with ministers like Roland—who had instituted the inquiry against Michel and Francois—relaxing controls and allowing grain-prices to soar, despite the opposition of Robespierre and his Jacobin associates, who warned them of the dangers of inflation, it was only persuasion on the part of Pierre that prevented Michel from leaving us and throwing in his lot with the extremists in Paris.*

Mitford's longest sentence is 68 words:

"Darling Sophia," he said, as she came to the end of a real tour

*de force about her father, whom she had left, she said, blackening
the pebbles of his drive which he considered would be particularly
visible from the air, "I know what your job will be in the war—
taking German spies out to lunch and telling them what you
believe to be the truth."*

(It is probably evident that both the DuMaurier and Mitford books are
historical novels, a genre perhaps lending itself to lengthier sentences.
But Mary Renault's book, *The Persian Boy,* is also an historical novel—
with an average sentence length of only 14 words.) DuMaurier's shortest sentence consists of three words; Mitford's, of ten words.

A frequency distribution of the sentence lengths in fiction indicates
that the specific examples given above *do* indicate the wider range in
men's fiction (see Table 3):

Table 3. Frequency Distribution of Sentence Lengths: Fiction Sample

Sentence Length (words)	No. of Instances— Men	No. of Instances— Women
1- 5	316	340
6- 10	754	752
11- 15	613	650
16- 20	503	484
21- 25	325	324
26- 30	236	212
31- 35	128	142
36- 40	83	73
41- 50	59	85
51- 60	25	78
61- 70	10	11
71- 80	6	5
81- 90	8	5
91-100	4	0
Over 100	2	0

The women, it would seem, write more "long" but not "very long" sentences than do the men, if one considers sentences of 41 to 60 words "long." In that range, their writing contains 163 instances, versus only 84 in the men's writing. Their writing also contains more sentences in the 1- to 15-word range–1742 versus 1683 for the men–although the difference is not nearly so pronounced as in the 41- 60-word range.

The comparatively shorter range of sentence length for the women fiction writers is supported by the fact that their *average* lengths vary by only ten words–from a low of 13 to a high of 23 words–whereas the men's averages vary by 17 words–from a low of 13 also, but to a high of 30.

Given the nature of the genre, patterns of sentence complexity in fiction are not particularly revealing, although there do exist considerable asyndeton and polysyndeton in fiction, a matter that will be discussed subsequently.

Summary

In both non-fiction and fiction, the sentence lengths of women writers are different from those of men.

Women's non-fiction sentences are shorter than men's, and the complexity of their sentences is more varied, with fewer repetitious patterns. The average length of women's fiction sentences is the same as men's, but their range of sentence length is not so wide as that of the men.

It is probably fair to state that women's sentences are less "extreme" than men's when it comes to sentence length and complexity–less "extreme" because less fixed in types of complexity and less "extreme" because less wide-ranging in length.

As far as sentence length is concerned, there is no justification whatsoever for believing that the "masculine" style is terse and the "feminine" style is verbose. If anything, the opposite is true.

Chapter 4

Who Is Scatterbrained?

The polar opposites in stereotyped male thinking—the silly little feather-headed woman and the sensible, profound, rational man—might be expected to reveal themselves in their writing. If such types do generally exist, the prose of women should exhibit excitability, emotionality, simplicity, confusion, and illogic, whereas the prose of men should manifest calmness, orderliness, profundity, and logic. Those aspects of the prose of men and women that might shed light on these notions should be examined.

One relatively simple yardstick for assessment of these qualities is certain types of punctuation. The use of the exclamation point, for example, generally indicates emotion of one sort or another—surprise, shock, indignation, fear, pleasure. It is not considered a "neutral" punctuator. This is not to say that sudden emotion is evidenced *only* by exclamation, for actual words can obviously perform the same function. A writer may choose to say something like "Jim was suddenly gripped by icy terror," or "Jane was overwhelmed by the unexpected gift." But it is nonetheless true that a writer may also choose to write "'My God!' said Jim, upon opening the door," or "'What a surprise!' exclaimed Jane."

Nonetheless, the frequency of use of exclamation points is one indicator of what might be called "emotionality" or "excitability" in writing. Women writers, according to stereotype, should therefore use more of this punctuation than do men writers. Such, however, is not the case.

Non-fiction

In non-fiction, the men use half again as many exclamation points as do the women. There are 42 in the men's sample and 28 in the women's sample. But only 11 of the 25 men writers use exclamations; 14 of the 25 women use them. The men writers would seem, therefore, to use them relatively frequently or not at all.

One might expect that the occurrence of exclamation points is heaviest in autobiographies and biographies because they contain more dialogue than other non-fiction. But again such is not the case. Among the male biographers, Rosten's *Marilyn* contains four exclamation points and Carey's *Brando!* contains three (not counting, of course, the exclamatory title). In Rosten's four exclamations, only one utterance is attributed to a woman: Marilyn Monroe says, "I'm ready, C.B., if you are!" Another is Rosten's own "Wow!" Two of Carey's exclamations are ascribed to Brando's former wife ("I'm not through fighting!"); the third is contained in a film title.

Among the women, Lindbergh's autobiography contains five exclamation points and may be counted as "dialogue" exclamations or representations of her own speech, such as "Gosh, what a channel that is!" and "Oh, it is so brutal!"

Almost all of the exclamation points do portray emotion, but since Rosten, Carey, and Lindbergh are only three of the 50 non-fiction authors, it cannot be claimed that biography and autobiography are generally more "exclamatory" in style than is other non-fiction, as can be seen in Table 4. If we consider that the use of four or more exclamation points in a 2000-word sample of writing can be termed at least a somewhat "exclamatory" style, we find that five of the male non-fiction writers and two of the female non-fiction writers employ such a style. Each of these seven writers uses the exclamation point somewhat differently, but always to express amazement, surprise, shock, etc.

Mailer's exclamations occur only as evidence of his own expostulation (and perhaps indignation) about something that might not be regarded as appropriate to such emotions:

Now, just as hippies might owe their lunar air to the consumption

Table 4. Occurrence of Exclamation Points: Non-Fiction

Male Author	Number	Female Author	Number
Rosten	4	Brothers	2
Carey	3	Farmer	1
Lash	2	Oakley	1
Thompson	1	Gordon	2
Peter	1	LeShan	7
Mander	1	Morgan	1
Mailer	4	Maynard	1
Edwards	9	Schreiber	1
Ellis	11	Lindbergh	5
Goodavage	5	Friday	2
Mankiewicz	1	Holmes	1
		Cartland	1
		Cohen	2
		DeMille	1
11 men	42	14 women	28

of the soul (and worse! the soul of futures unborn) in the fires of mystical states they had not earned. . . .

. . . there had been a power failure in the Mission Control Center at Houston, in the Mission Control Center! One could not get nearer to the center of the technical brain.

How their faces must have looked in that deep boudoir light! Then the power came back.

. . . the very real interface between physics and engineering. Interface! perhaps it was the biggest word at NASA.

In the case of Frank Edwards' use of the exclamation point, however, most of the exclamation points occur in dialogue, but always the spoken utterances of men, not women:

"There's your killer, gentlemen! You will find him in British Columbia!"

"I've located your car," he exclaimed, "but you'll have to hurry before the thief gets away!"

"Go that way!" he exclaimed.

. . . Roberts shouted "The car is coming toward us! Turn around and we'll follow it!"

Kores, the taxi driver who had been slugged and robbed yelled: "That's it, Warren!"

"That's my cab and that's the guy who slugged me!"

Two instances from Edwards' sample occur in a non-dialogue situation:

Not only that lesson but every lesson in the book!

On the green slip of paper were the questions and cuneiform texts identical to those he had seen in his strange dreams a few hours before!

Albert Ellis' comparatively frequent use of the exclamation point is likewise contained in the representation of male *(not female)* speech. A few examples will suffice, for the subject matter is repetitive:

"I should be able to be perfectly potent with almost any attractive women, especially Gloria, and I'm a shit if I'm not!"

"How awful it is that I failed!"

"I might as well kill myself!"

"I'll never be able to succeed, now that she doesn't like me!"

Ellis comments on his male clients at one point as follows:

> *Well! By telling themselves crap like this, these men would natu-rally be "traumatized."*

The remaining male author to use four or more exclamation points in his sample is Joseph Goodavage. He does not use them in dialogue, but in his own reporting of an astronomical occurrence, always with a sense of shock and surprise:

> *The solar system actually stretches through a tremendous area of space reaching five-sixths of the way to the closest star!*

> *It has been going on for centuries—for millenia!*

> *By some staggering "coincidence," the same thing had happened at the same place exactly a century before!*

> *Or even an x-ray machine!*

> *For him it would be years before the incandescent lamp would be more than just a novelty!*

As for the women who use four or more exclamation points in their samples, the nature of their use by Anne Lindbergh has already been discussed. Eda LeShan, however, uses seven exclamation points, the highest incidence by the women, but lower than that of two of the men. Two of the exclamation points occur in speech attributed to a man (e.g., "One is living in sin in San Francisco and the other is living in sin in New York!"), two to a woman (e.g., "The girl is just a little bit pregnant!"), and three do not occur in dialogue and are thus part of LeShan's own style:

> *Their lack of concern for money would seem more admirable if it were money they earned instead of ours!*

Too often we play right into behavior that drives us crazy!

Just because Mr. Rockefeller was rich, didn't seem to make him think he had to give his children a lot of money!

In summary, both the women non-fiction writers who use four or more exclamation points in their writing do seem to use this form of punctuation mainly as an aspect of their own style, especially Anne Lindbergh. Lindbergh's occur in her own first-person, informal narrative, whereas LeShan's are divided among representations of male speech, representations of female speech, and her own statements. As for the men, Rosten's four exclamation points occur only once in representation of female speech. The other three instances are functions of his own style. Mailer's exclamation points likewise occur as a matter of his own style, as do Goodavage's. The majority of the exclamation points in Edwards' and Ellis' samples, however, occur in the representation of *male* speech.

The significant point here is that those male non-fiction writers who use a relatively high number of exclamation points use them as facets of either their *own* style or the style of *male* speech. The Ellis and Edwards samples, as a matter of fact, contain male exclamations that sound positively hysterical.

In general, the women's use of the exclamation point is more widely and more evenly spread. Fewer men use the exclamation point than the women, but those who do, use it far more often. It is thus unquestionable that the women writers as a group do *not* exclaim more often than the men. If exclamations usually mean excitement, surprise, thrill, "hysteria," etc., the women are more moderate in their expression of these feelings than the men.

Another type of punctuation that might be thought of as almost the "opposite" of the exclamation point is the parenthesis, for the parenthesis generally indicates non-essential, "afterthought," or incidental material not in any way associated with strong feeling. An investigation of this type of punctuation reveals a different, but not really inconsistent, pattern as compared to the use of the exclamation point. For if parentheses indicate non-essential material, then the women non-fiction writers certainly seem to feel that more of what they say is, in a sense, disposable. Of the 25 writers, 19 use 106 parenthetical expressions, whereas 19 of the 25 men use only 79. The women thus use parenthesis 25 percent more often than do the men (see Table 5).

Table 5. Use of Parentheses: Non-Fiction

Male Author	Number	Female Author	Number
Rosten	4	FitzGerald	4
Carey	5	Chesler	12
Lash	1	Brothers	4
Thompson	2	Farmer	1
Salisbury	6	Oakley	2
Bing	9	Gordon	1
Cartwright	2	Morgan	1
Plimpton	5	Houston	14
Peter	2	Maynard	20
Rovere	2	Schreiber	1
Mander	8	Lindbergh	8
Taylor	4	Friday	6
Mailer	6	Vilar	3
Toffler	1	Holmes	5
Edwards	1	Millett	5
Ellis	7	Cohen	4
Goodavage	6	Hodges	4
Mankiewicz	3	Sanders	4
Greene	5	DeMille	7
Total	79	Total	106

The use of parenthetical expressions by the 38 authors ranges in frequency from one such expression to 20. With such a span, it seems reasonable to study in some detail what might be called the "high" users, or those with more than six parenthetical expressions in their samples.

It is immediately evident that three of the women writers use parentheses more often than any of the men: Houston, Maynard, and Chesler. Two other women, Lindbergh and DeMille, use seven and eight parentheses respectively. Three male writers use more than six parentheses: Bing, Mander, and Ellis.

Chesler's use of parenthesis seems to follow no particular pattern. Sometimes entire sentences are parenthetical; sometimes words that one would deem necessary are nonetheless enclosed in parentheses. An example of each type of use will suffice:

> *(As we shall see, both their medical training and their legal responsibility predispose most psychiatrists to diagnose "pathology" everywhere—even, or especially, where non-experts are blind to it.)*

> *Dr. Charles Dahlberg presents the seductive therapist as a man who chose to practice psychotherapy between 1930 and 1943 and who was probably withdrawn and introspective, studious, passive, shy, (more) intellectually (than) physically adventurous among other things. . . .*

Houston's use of parenthesis, on the other hand, is more consistent. Almost all film titles as references for particular scenes are enclosed in parentheses; other parenthetical material consists of phrases apparently considered non-essential:

> *Richardson can do some things so well (the theatrical things, as might be expected from his background) that one wonders . . . .*

> *The films he makes will be much more rigidly categorized than anything produced in the West: within the two basic divisions of the Jidai-Geki (period subject) and the Gendai-Geki (modern subject), are the endless subdivisions. . . .*

Maynard's high usage is akin to one aspect of Chesler's usage; entire sentences are enclosed in parentheses, although they do not seem to contain either irrelevant or non-essential material:

> (Like the kids who, as late as twelfth grade, would hold up College boards by asking . . . .)

> (They brandished their razors; we hid ours.)

> (The mediator's role always seemed an odd one to me. . . .)

> (Going to church was OK, like going to Brownies. But to speak, as Ralphie Leveque did, of loving God and of the Blood of Christ, and Mary's tears and thorns and nails—that seemed almost dirty.)

Maynard also uses parenthetical phrases, however, in relative abundance:

> Hands were always a problem that way . . . not crossing them (too tough) or putting them on your hips (too I-dare-you), or . . . .

> . . . the author of any slim volume of austere prose or poetry (the fewer words he writes, the more profound each one must be) . . . .

Lindbergh once employs double parentheses:

> The first and most common offerings of family and friends are always distractions ("Take her out"—"Get her away"—"Change the scene"—"Bring in people to cheer her up"—"Don't let her sit and mourn" (when it is mourning one needs.))

and several times places parentheses around complete sentences:

> Daddy had died since last year, and the baby (I'm glad he lived in this beauty for a while). . . .

> *But C. knows enough about it to make it go (He did before, you know, as a boy).*

DeMille also uses her parentheses mainly to enclose complete sentences, as in the following:

> *(I quickly found that a nice little bed could be made on the floor with sofa cushions.)*

> *(Naturally neither Freddy nor I could afford a Mayfair lunch.)*

> *("Oh," he said, "I think so, easily, easily, and several moving pictures and operas.")*

> *(She felt the same way about Anthony.)*

> *(Martha Graham did not pay her girls for years.)*

Of the three male non-fiction writers who use more than six parenthetical expressions, Bing tends to enclose entire sentences rather than phrases in parentheses:

> *(As I said in my first statement to the New York press, I wanted an "ensemble of stars, not of comets"). . . .*

> *(In the fall, before the Metropolitan call and audition, . . . I heard Mario Del Monaco, whom I not only engaged . . . but also invited. . . . It was a mistake: The critics resented the idea of a guest, and I got him to do it too cheaply; I paid him $150 or $250 for the evening, I've forgotten which, and he never forgave me for it.)*

One can seriously question the parenthetical nature of the last example, containing as it does several sentences involving his own activities and his own power. The parentheses perhaps connote false modesty.

Mander, on the other hand, makes a full sentence parenthetical only twice in his sample:

> *(This is the phenomenon Da Cunha describes in "Rebellion in the Backlands.")*

> *(Mexico City is credited with the highest murder rate in the world.)*

His other six instances consist of phrases or dependent clauses.

None of Ellis' parentheses encloses sentences. The following are typical:

> *. . . or any set of preferences (usually or regularly). . . .*

> *. . . has the trait of sensuousness for him (and other men who have his kissing preferences). . . .*

> *. . . these kinds of techniques (which are frequently used by Masters and Johnson). . . .*

> *. . . Dr. Reuben (and his writings) . . . .*

In general, then, not only do women use parenthetical expressions more often than do men, but they also enclose more complete sentences in parentheses than do the men. Houston and Bing are the two exceptions; she does not enclose complete sentences; he does. More of the women, then, regard more of their words as non-essential.

If this pattern is regarded as a form of self-abnegation, it is consistent with the relatively non-exclamatory nature of their sentences. Along with the comparative *lack* of excitability occurs a sense of unimportance.

This impression is borne out by the fact that those writers who use a relatively high number of exclamation points are *not* the same as those who use a relatively high number of parentheses—with one exception,

Albert Ellis. A comparative tabulation of the two types of punctuation is given in Table 6.

Table 6. Authors with "High" Use of Exclamation Points and Parentheses

Exclamation Point[a] Author	Number	Parentheses[b] Author	Number
Rosten	4	Bing	9
Mailer	4	Mander	8
Edwards	9	Ellis	7
Ellis	11	Chesler	12
Goodavage	5	Houston	14
LeShan	7	Maynard	20
Lindbergh	5	DeMille	7
(five males, two females)		(three males, four females)	

[a]Four or more per sample.
[b]Seven or more per sample.

Another form of punctuation, the dash, serves a somewhat different, although at times overlapping, function from the use of the parenthesis. In general, the dash is a less formal type of punctuation, indicating asides, random thoughts, interruptions of thought, but also conclusions and exemplifications. The dash, of course, may be used singly, or doubly to "enclose" words or phrases. The "single" dash indicates rather more informality than does the "double" dash, for the latter functions as a less constricting parenthesis. Part of the underlying reason for the informal style connoted by the dash is that it is often used instead of more standard punctuation; and part of the reason is that mentioned above—that the material set off by the dash is often a type of afterthought or random comment.

The total number of dashes used by the men and women non-fiction writers is not significantly different, but the nature of the dashes (i.e., the single versus the pseudoparenthetical, "double" dash) does vary somewhat. A frequency distribution is given in Table 7.

Table 7. Use of the Dash: Non-Fiction

Men				Women		
Author	Single	"Double"	Total	Author	Single	"Double"	Total
Rosten	3	6	9	FitzGerald	6	2	8
Carey	4	3	7	Chesler	9	2	11
Maas	1	2	3	Brothers	2	2	4
Pilat	0	3	3	Farmer	1	0	1
Thompson	12	8	20	Oakley	1	0	1
Salisbury	5	2	7	LeShan	23	5	28
Clark	1	0	1	Morgan	1	0	1
Bing	7	1	8	Montgomery	0	1	1
Cartwright	1	0	1	Houston	1	2	3
Plimpton	11	5	16	Howar	3	0	3
Peter	4	0	4	Maynard	19	5	24
Rovere	2	1	3	Schreiber	1	2	3
Mander	5	6	11	Lindbergh	17	4	21
Mailer	5	3	8	Friday	5	5	10
Belz	2	1	3	Vilar	6	1	7
Toffler	7	0	7	Steiner	1	0	1
Edwards	9	2	11	Holmes	5	3	8
Ellis	12	4	16	Cartland	3	0	3
Goodavage	6	1	7	Millett	2	0	2
Mankiewicz	8	6	14	Cohen	1	0	1
Greene	6	1	7	Fisher	7	4	11
Taylor	1	1	2	Hodges	6	1	7
				Sanders	3	8	11
				DeMille	8	1	9
22 men	112	56	168	24 women	131	48	179

Although 24 women use at least one dash in their samples, as compared to 22 men, their use of the single dash is nonetheless a bit higher than that of the men. The average "single dash occurrence" for the 22 men is 5.09, whereas the average "single dash occurrence" for the 24 women is 5.45. This slight difference is reversed in the use of the "double" dash; the men's average "double dash occurrence" is 2.54 and the women's, 2. There seems, therefore, a tendency to more embedded comment on the part of the men and a tendency toward a looser, more casual comment on the part of the women.

More significant perhaps is the fact that the "high" dash users of both sexes always use the single dash more often than the "double" dash. The dash-prone writer of either sex adds more afterthoughts, random comments, and details than he or she embeds within the sentence.

The difference in range of occurrence is also noteworthy. In the women's prose, the dash occurs in the 21 samples from 1 to 28 times; LeShan (28) and Maynard and Lindbergh (each 24) can be called the "high" users. In the 22 men's prose, the range is from 1 to 20, with Thompson (20) the highest and Plimpton and Ellis each using 16.

Some exemplification of the use of dashes by the three male and three female authors who use them most often might serve to indicate differences.

Hunter Thompson:

> *One of the main marks of success in a career politician is a rooty distrust of the press—and this cynicism is usually reciprocated, in spades, by most reporters who have . . . .*

> *. . . and in two hours I have to lash my rum-soaked red convertible across the Rickenbacker Causeway to downtown Miami and then to the airport—in order to meet John Lindsay in either Tallahassee or Atlanta, depending . . . .*

> *. . . they said they hadn't got around to making any decision on it yet—but I probably wouldn't be needing that one either.*

> *. . . then McGovern should be there too—or Hubert might say his distinguished opponent cared more about winning the Nebraska primary than avoiding World War Three.*

He wasn't much; they all agreed on that—but by May he was all they had left.

A McGovern/Kennedy ticket would, after all, put Nixon in deep trouble from the start—and it would also give Teddy . . . .

George Plimpton:

. . . and Billingham went up to his bedroom to take a nap— the Aaron confrontation the next day just barely on the edge of his consciousness and making him yawn.

. . . Bowie Kuhn made it quite clear that he expected the Braves to play Aaron in two of the three games in Cincinnati—his view was that it was imperative that the public believe . . . .

The hotel is full of funeral directors—a convention of them, wearing their name tags in plastic covers.

It reminds me of Atlanta on the same night of the Quarry-Ali fight some years ago—the same frisson of anticipation.

Albert Ellis:

A good many men are poor kissers—and great lovers otherwise.

Certainly a slobbery man isn't sensual—for a non-slobbery woman.

But a human being is not anything—except, perhaps, just that: a human being.

It's merely unpleasant and unfortunate—and it shows that Gloria has quite a problem if she puts me down for failing.

Joyce Maynard:

> *Mrs. Logan, the nurse who came to speak to our class, was the same one who delivered me when I was born (an additional shame—she'd seen me naked).*

> *It wasn't the facts I objected to—sex education I certainly applaud.*

> *And then there were bras, and the dilemma—when to buy one, what kind, when to wear it and with Kleenex stuffed inside or not.*

> *. . . to be drenched in holy waters after a drug-filled adolescence, a form of the new nostalgia, even—almost camp.*

Anne Lindbergh:

> *And then stopping the boat to listen for bells and horns—to guide yourself by that alone.*

> *It will all have to be done under someone else's name and the publicity run on a false place—the second break won't be as great.*

> *It is like being born with no nose, or deformed—everyone on the street looks at you once and then again; always looked back—that second look, the leer.*

> *One must guard and protect the new life growing within—like a child.*

Eda LeShan:

> *We don't really want to be left behind—left out.*

> *I think we recognize that we have a serious choice to make—not*

*only in relation to changing attitudes about sex, but social cus-
toms and values in general.*

*. . . as partners with younger people, we will be allowed—perhaps
even encouraged and asked—to point out these fundamental and
eternal verities that do not change, that have validity and
meaning—that give hope and purpose and meaning to life—
despite change.*

*Each year more and more young people remain financially de-
pendent on their parents for a longer period of time—until it is not
at all ususual for adults of 25 and older to still be in school.*

The ways that the dashes, especially the single dashes, are used by the
men and the women are structually undifferentiated, with the possible
exception of Hunter Thompson, who uses them fairly consistently to
delineate complete sentences. The men's dashes, however, are perhaps
more "conclusive" than those of the women, for in the case of the male
writers, the dash instead of the comma serves to emphasize the words
following the dash. With the women writers, the dash more often
serves to introduce added comment that is not always emphatic but is
often a rewording or an exemplification.

The emphatic or conclusive aspect of the material following the
men's dashes is reflected in a study of the logical sequence of their
arguments as compared with that of the women. The stereotyped
woman is "illogical," as we all know, but in fact the women are just as
logical as the men, although their patterns of logic are different from
the men's.

Sentence and paragraph connectives (the modification of a list previously devised by Louis T. Milic[1]) are helpful in revealing the manner
in which writers develop their ideas and arguments. Such connectives,
or "logical sequence indicators," are divided into five groups:

1. Illustratives. These are words that serve to introduce examples and
   illustrations of a previous statement, such as "for example," "that
   is," "for instance."

2. Illatives. These are words that indicate that a concluding statement is being made, such as "therefore," "(and) so," "thus," "hence," and "in conclusion."
3. Adversatives. Adversatives serve to signal a reversal in the direction of the argument or to introduce an antithetical statement, by means of words or phrases like "however," "but," "nevertheless," "on the other hand."
4. Causatives. These words indicate that a reason or justification for a preceding statement is being offered, as in the use of "because," "for," and "since."
5. Additives. These are words that introduce further information or argument, more facts, as it were, concerning the topic. They include "and" and "so . . . did."

These logical sequence indicators are just that—they are isolated words or phrases that imply certain logical processes. That there are other ways of indicating a line of argument is undeniable, but use of the indicators in a certain amount of exposition is almost unavoidable. It seems cogent, therefore, to study these indicators despite the fact that a logical argument does not entirely depend on them.

The women non-fiction writers use 190 logical sequence indicators in the samples from their 25 books, whereas the men use 160. By no stretch of the imagination, therefore, can it be said that women write less logically than do men. But examination of the different types of indicators used by each group does reveal significant difference in the type of logic each group tends to use.

The men, for instance, use illustratives 50 percent more frequently than do the women. One could expect their arguments to be buttressed by exemplification more often than those of the women. The men also use illatives 50 percent more often than do the women; it can be said, therefore, that they reach more conclusions than do the women. This particular finding is not surprising in view of the "conclusive" nature of the material following their dashes, as commented on above.

Both groups use almost exactly the same number of adversatives. Both, in other words, probably offer antithetical or opposing statements equally often. The reversed argument of course does not indicate a cancelling out of argument, for if Statement A is made, following by "but" Statement B, it is Statement B that the author is supporting. The use of adversatives usually indicates a rhetorical stratagem.

The women, on the other hand, use causatives and additives 50 percent more often than do the men. Thus it is probably valid to say that they offer more reasons and justification for their statements than do the men and that they also add more information, more "points," to their arguments.

With the use of adversatives as neutral, the reverse proportions of illustratives and illatives versus causatives and additives is striking. For the women, fewer conclusions, fewer examples, more added information, and, above all, more reasons would indicate that the women's logic is more self-justifying and less inclined to be definitive than that of the men. The men's comparatively high use of illustratives and illatives suggests a basis for the so-called authoritative tone of men's writing.

Nonetheless, the women are not illogical; they are only differently logical. On the basis of the particular aspects of style investigated in this chapter, the women are not "scatterbrained." They neither expostulate nor exclaim so often as do the men. The structure of their prose, given its relatively shorter sentences, is quite possibly easier to understand and clearer than that of the men. They do not go to extremes of length and verbosity. If they regard more of what they say as non-essential, as indicated by their more frequent use of parentheses, they are also comparatively reluctant to reach conclusions. If these findings point to a less than "authoritative" style, so be it. Their non-fiction prose is generally more conservative, more cautious, and less emotional than is that of the men.

Fiction

As contrasted with the differences found in the non-fiction of the men and the women, in the category of fiction there is absolutely no difference between the two groups in any of the aspects of style commented on in this chapter. That is, the women writers of fiction are neither more nor less "exclamatory" than the men; the women's use of parenthesis is the same as the men's, as is their use of the dash. (The study of logical sequence indicators was not undertaken for the fiction sample on the ground that the process of argumentation and the development of logical patterns are unrelated to the purposes of fiction.)

The similarity of the men's and women's fiction writing is all the more amazing when one considers that the genre of fiction consists of several sub-genres, such as the mystery novel (written primarily by men) and the Gothic novel (written primarily by women). The similarity of these aspects of style in general fiction overrides any distinctions based on the sex of the writer.

Summary

In considering the fact that most literary critics deal with fiction when making their appraisals of "feminine" or "masculine" style, one can only conclude that the critics are basing their opinions on something other than those aspects of style thus far discussed, for the real differences emerge in non-fiction, rather than in fiction. In non-fiction, the women exclaim less frequently, regard more of what they say as dispensable, are somewhat likely to add on new ideas rather than reach conclusions. Their logic is different from that of the male writers in that they tend to support their arguments with reasons rather than illustrations and to use "extra" information rather than conclusions. In fiction, the two groups do not diverge as far as these particular aspects of style are concerned.

Chapter 5

The Well-Balanced Writer

Mary Ellman points out that insane or "unbalanced" male writers are generally regarded as creative and inspired, whereas "unbalanced" women are simply regarded as sick or incompetent, or "shrill," "hysterical," and the like.[1] One male critic, Leo Lowenthal, even refers to a woman whose speech is entirely "lucid" but who is "obviously insane."[2] These are, of course, references to psychic states, and we are talking of writing style. But if disordered speech is a symptom of a disordered mind, it is not unreasonable to assume that disordered writing is likewise a product of a disordered mind. A disordered, confused psychic state can obviously be indicated in several linguistic modes, in inappropriate or "meaningless" words and phrases as well as in collapse of syntactic structure. Parallelism in written style is only one type of syntactic order, and its presence or absence as evidence of the condition of the psyche can only be a moot point. Nonetheless, it is women's writing that is deemed lacking in order, as compared with the rational, orderly style of men. A study of the parallel structures occurring in the writing of the two groups quite possibly might reveal that yet another male-derived myth is without foundation, for parallelism is evidence of balance and control in a prose style.

Parallelism may be defined as two or more words or structurally similar groups of words that serve the same syntactic function in a sentence, such as two or more nouns serving as the subject of a sentence, or two or more prepositional phrases modifying the same noun, or two or more clauses serving as the object. Those parallelisms of individual words may be termed "simple" parallelisms; those involving phrases and clauses may be called "complex."[3] For example, the sentence "They enjoy swimming, sailing, and diving" contains three verb forms as the object of the main verb "enjoy," and therefore is a sentence containing a simple parallel construction.

The writer using parallel forms likes a neat, orderly sentence, likes equally weighted constructions, and likes the emphasis supplied by the repetition of a pattern. A ride on his or her sentence is like a train ride—relatively smooth, fairly straight, reasonably predictable, and on safe, parallel tracks.

Prose that does not contain much parallelism, however, is akin to a plane flight—smooth or rough (depending on downdrafts), direct or circuitous (depending on thunderheads and other planes), reasonably predictable only at certain times, but by contrast to the train, exciting, chancey, and unconnected with any visible, obligatory tracks.

Train travel can be tediously boring; plane travel can be chaotic. Parallelism is essentially a bulwark against stylistic chaos, but too much can be stultifying. Order and balance, to be effective and interesting, must be broken with or interrupted by disorder and imbalance. Order and disorder exist only in the context of each other. Balance is meaningless, as well as boring, without imbalance.

With regard to parallelism, two questions may be asked concerning the men and women writers in this study. Who are actually the more "orderly" and "balanced," the men or the women? And which group is more *effectively* "orderly" and "balanced"? Or, to put the questions another way, do women use more parallel constructions than men and do they use them more persuasively?

Despite the relatively simple definition offered earlier, parallelism is a rather complicated matter. Many parallelisms, for instance, are dictated by linguistic necessity, such as the simple doublet (two items), "bacon and eggs." Such linguistically necessary pairs have little or nothing to do with a writer's style, for there is no other way to say them—they are, in effect, inescapable.

Many other parallel constructions are composed of rather long, complicated doublets where any sense of parallelism is almost nonexistent. A long compound sentence, for example, with many modifiers, may follow a "perfectly" parallel pattern consisting of Adverbial-Subject-Verb-Object "and" Adverbial-Subject-Verb-Object. If, however, the individual components of such a sentence are themselves varying in structure or heavily modified, as in a sentence where the first subject is a clause and the second is a nominal modified by a clause, with variation also in the structure of the object, then the basic parallel structure of the sentence is imperceptible. Thus:

> *Occasionally the old warlords had managed to transform themselves into emperors or Mandarins, but they had the traditional Confucian system to fall back on.* (FitzGerald; *Fire in the Lake*)

The sentence offers the reader little sense of parallel construction because of the variation within the structure of the two objects. This type of sentence is also of little stylistic value, for although the parallelism is not "obligatory," as are the linguistically necessary pairs commented on above, it contains too much variation for the reader to perceive any pattern. Both of these "non-stylistic" types of parallelism occur very frequently in all prose and are not regarded here as worthy of close study.

A more general examination of parallelism, however, including those "non-stylistic" occurrences, reveals that the men and women writers employ almost equal amounts. In non-fiction, 57 percent of the men's sentences contain at least one instance of parallelism; 54 percent of the women's non-fiction sentences contain at least one parallel construction. The difference in range of occurrence among the authors is also only slightly less for the women. The male authors' samples contain from 32 percent (Maas) to 74 percent (Taylor); the women's range is from 38 percent (Vilar) to 70 percent (FitzGerald).

The slightly less frequent use of parallelism by the women is reversed in the fiction category: 46 percent of the women's sentences contain at least one parallelism versus 44 percent of the men's. But in fiction, as in non-fiction, the range of occurrence is slightly greater among the men: from 25 percent (Carlino) to 78 percent (Burgess) versus 33 percent

(Didion) to 71 percent (Newman). The lower incidence of parellelism in fiction is simply a reflection of genre and confirms my previous study. What these figures indicate is that the men's and women's writing styles are almost equally balanced in terms of parallelism. Therefore, in answer to the first question posed earlier, the women do *not* use more parallel constructions than the men; they use approximately the same number.

But, as in the case of other aspects of writing style previously discussed, there are some important differences that are not revealed in gross averages. These differences reside in the specific types of parallel constructions utilized by each group. If all the obligatory simple doublets and hazy, imprecise complex doublets are removed from consideration, and if our attention is focused on the rhetorical devices of repetition that may co-occur with the other, less common types of parallelism, differences definitely emerge.

There are two phrases that need clarification: "rhetorical devices of repetition" and "other, less common types of parallelism." The rhetorical devices of repetition consist of certain repetitions of words or sounds for emphasis, or for, as some rhetoricians put it, "persuasiveness." Alliteration is one of the most commonly known of these devices, consisting as it does of the repetition of a sound at the beginning of words. At times, these devices occur in a parallel construction, and when they do, they reinforce its effectiveness immeasurably. The specific rhetorical devices found in this study co-occurring with a parallel construction are as follows:

1. Alliteration—recurrence of the same initial sound, usually a consonant.
2. Anaphora—repetition of the same word or words at the beginning of phrases or clauses in sequence.
3. Antithesis—juxtaposition of contrasting or opposing ideas.
4. Asyndeton—omission of conjunctions in triplets and series.
5. Epistrophe—ending of phrases or clauses with the same word or words, when the phrases or clauses are in parallel sequence.
6. Homoioteleuton—similar endings of words in sequence.

7. Pleonasm—use of more than one word in a context when one word is enough.
8. Polysyndeton—repetitive use of conjunctions in triplets or series.
9. Syllepsis—use of one verb with a literal subject or object plus a figurative subject or object.
10. Tmesis—repetition of a word with one or a few words in between.

As for the "other, less common types of parallelism," what is meant is simply those kinds of parallel constructions, simple or complex, that occur relatively infrequently in prose and that are readily perceived as parallelisms. The triplet, a parallel construction involving three segments, does not occur, for example, nearly so often as does the doublet and is easily perceived. Series are less often used than triplets and are thus even more noticeable. These constructions do involve stylistic choice and are noteworthy even when they are not reinforced by any of the aforementioned devices of repetition. When they are supplemented by one of the devices of repetition, they are highly emphatic and effective.

A triplet or series reinforced by either polysyndeton or asyndeton, for instance, is highly effective because of the nature of the two rhetorical devices. Both polysyndeton and asyndeton create an element of uncertainty as to when a triplet or series will end. "Cola, ginger ale, soda, and root beer" is what might be called a normal parallel series, with its conclusion signaled by the "and." But both "cola and ginger ale and soda and root beer" and "cola, ginger ale, soda, root beer" are constructions that leave some doubt as to when the series is ended; there are either "too many" conjunctions or "not enough." In this way, polysyndeton and asyndeton call special attention to the seriation.

Several basic types of parallelism are studied, excluding the "nonstylistic" types commented on previously. These include (1) simple and (2) complex doublets, but only those *reinforced* by one of the rhetorical devices of repetition, (3) simple and (4) complex triplets, and (5) simple and (6) complex series, all with or without co-occurring devices of repetition. Each of these basic types can be further subdivided according to their co-occurrence with one or more of the specific rhetorical devices. The subdivision provides an extended list of types of parallelism. For example, a complex doublet with anaphora is one type occurring on the extended list; a simple triplet is another; a complex, asyndetic triplet is still another, as is a polysyndetic complex series.

Non-Fiction

A tabulation of the basic types in the non-fiction sample without specifying either the nature of or the presence or absence of a reinforcing rhetorical device is given in Table 8.

Table 8. Basic Types of Parallelism: Non-Fiction

Type	Instances in Men's Sample	Instances in Women's Sample
Simple doublet	207	182
Complex doublet	81	85
Simple triplet	64	105
Complex triplet	44	70
Simple series	53	41
Complex series	30	48
Total	479	531

Although the men employ less parallelism of the "basic" types than do the women, their sample contains approximately the same number of simple parallelisms (324) as does the women's sample (328). Hence, the women use more of the complex structures. Furthermore, if we recall that the women and men non-fiction writers use almost the same amount of parallelism when the instances include occurrences of the "non-stylistic" variety and observe that the women use *more* parallelism when the "non-stylistic" parallelisms are not considered, we can only conclude that the men's use of parallelism is not so often a matter of style as is the women's. The women's style, therefore, is more "balanced" than the men's.

This finding is consistent with the results of investigation of the "extended" list of types of parallelism, that is, the basic types subdivided into those co-occurring with specific devices of repetition. Here we find that the men non-fiction writers employ 45 different combinations and that the women's writing contains 55 different combinations. Thus the women's constructions are more varied than those of the men.

A study of the specific rhetorical devices of repetition, whether in the context of doublets, triplets, or series, offers other major differences, as Table 9 indicates.

Table 9. Frequency of Rhetorical Devices of Repetition: Non-Fiction

Device	Instances in Men's Sample	Instances in Women's Sample
Polysyndeton	17	51
Asyndeton	58	88
Alliteration/ Homoioteleuton[a]	82	85
Anaphora	76	76
Antithesis	78	65
Syllepsis	2	2
Tmesis	0	1
Epistrophe	1	1

[a] These two devices are joined in the tabulation because they are concerned with the beginnings and endings of words, thus often involving rhyme.

The striking difference between the two groups is seen in the use of polysyndeton and asyndeton, where the women use precisely three times as many polysyndeta as the men, and approximately one-third again more asyndeta, and in the use of antithesis, which the men employ approximately one-sixth more often than the women.

Polysyndeton is found in the writing of 14 women and 12 men, or a little more than half of the women's non-fiction and a little less than half of the men's non-fiction. The male writer whose sample contains polysyndeton most frequently is Bing, who uses it four times. The other eleven men employ it either once or twice. But six of the women writers, on the other hand, use polysyndeton four or *more* times: Holmes (9), Lindbergh (8), Maynard (8), Morgan (5), DeMille (5), and Gordon (4). Thus there is a propensity on the part of the women who use polysyndeton at all to use it much more often than do the men. A few randomly chosen examples from the writing of these women illustrate the tone established by such a device.

Holmes:

> . . . *sunshine, and butter, and daffodils, and autumn trees.*

> . . . *in wallpapers and leathers and dyes.*

> . . . *shining and good and lovely.*

Maynard:

> . . . *space shots and wars and new music and new dances and new drugs.*

> . . . *they hung and swung and dangled and sweated* . . . .

> . . . *feet and hips and hair and tresses and ties and braces and, most of all, hands.*

Lindbergh:

> . . . *gape and giggle and spy on us.*

> . . . *stare and follow and giggle* . . . .

> . . . *as cold and as amazed and as insulting* . . . .

Morgan:

> *. . . rapture or exhaustion or even postcoital triestesse . . . .*

> *. . . too tall or too short or too black or too long-haired . . . .*

DeMille:

> *. . . daily household happenings are events, and the main reasons and dynamics of living are not, and the main goal is to be alive tomorrow morning.*

> *. . . with business and news and concern . . . .*

Gordon:

> *. . . all the hams and cakes and sandwiches . . . .*
> *. . . then he and Fay and the Blinns . . . .*

A predilection for polysyndeton lessens the opportunity for grammatical subordination, for if a string of items is joined equally by the same connective, there can be no hierarchical value assigned to the items. And the emphasis is the emphasis of unpredictability, for the reader does not know when the list will end. But it is also the emphasis of *sameness.* The effect is often one of childishness and naiveté, simply because no judgment is being made about the relative importance of the items. Each is equally "important." If one asks a small child what he or she did in kindergarten, one is often answered polysyndetically. In this respect, therefore, the style of many of the women non-fiction writers might seem somewhat childish and non-judgmental as compared with that of the men. The finding is not inconsistent with the comparatively low number of illatives (conclusions) used by the women non-fiction writers, as noted in Chapter 4.

With asyndeton, the element of unexpectedness likewise occurs, but not with the same repetitive flatness of polysyndeton, as can be seen in the following examples from both men's and women's non-fiction:

She would go through the ritual of disguise: glasses, sloppy dress, long scarf, no makeup or a mask makeup, flat shoes, outlandish hat. (Norman Rosten)

Olivier became impatient, edgy, martyred . . . . (Rosten)

. . . there had to be a way to separate them, blow them apart, cut all the communicating wires . . . . (Norman Mailer)

. . . you bought your food in the automatic vending machine room to avoid interface, the waitress coming up to your dinner table for the first time was interface, the taxicab driver to the new passenger, the cop to the kid he has just arrested, the boy making love to his girl—interface was at every joint . . . . (Mailer)

. . . his hand remains as steady, his humour as insolent, his mastery of the camera as complete . . . . (Penelope Houston)

. . . uniquely valuable assimilation of tradition—Kabuke, painting, literature—into the new art. (Houston)

And I was happy as though I had recovered them for a moment, as though I had recovered everything ever lost, as though I had everything . . . . (Anne Lindbergh)

. . . too highly charged, too naked, too close . . . . (Nancy Friday)

. . . we made it more mechanical, more rigid, more demanding. (Eda LeShan)

There is considerable variety among even these few examples, for the asyndeta range from the simple to the complex constructions and often include the added device of anaphora.

Nonetheless, by contrast with polysyndeton, the effect is one of terseness, of not wishing to waste words, despite the listing of several items. There is also a repetitive "hammer-blow" effect in asyndeton that

is in total contrast to the stringing-out effect of polysyndeton. Asyndeton is thus *not* childish; it is quite the opposite.

Twenty of the men use asyndeton; 19 of the women use that particular device. More men and women, therefore, use it than use polysyndeton, but again there are more women who use it more frequently than
do the men. Among the men, there are four who use asyndeton four or
more times: Mailer (11), Rosten (10), and Bing and Cartwright (4
each). All the others who employ asyndeton use it fewer than four
times. Of the women who employ asyndeton, there are twelve who use
it four or more times: Lindbergh (12), Houston (10), LeShan (7), Friday (7), Maynard (6), Howar, Holmes, and Millett (each 5 times), and
Chesler, Schreiber, and DeMille (each 4 times). Lindbergh, Maynard,
Holmes, and DeMille can be considered "high" users of both polysyndeton and asyndeton. Of the men, only Bing, with four instances of
each device, can be said to be a "high" user of both devices. As mentioned, both the men and the women use asyndeton more often than
polysyndeton, but the men use asyndeton more than three times as
often as they use polysyndeton, whereas the women use asyndeton only
1.7 times as often.

Thus, with regard to these two contrasting devices, the men do seem
definitely to prefer the impression of terseness and "hardness" conveyed
by asyndeton, and the women seem, once again, to balance the two,
with the naïve and childlike quality of polysyndeton poised against
driving, relentless quality of asyndeton.

There is, as has been noted, some difference between the men and the
women in the frequency of use of antithesis. The device itself is concerned with meaning rather than the structure, however, and thus
whether antithetical ideas are or are not being expressed depends largely
on the judgment of the reader, and it is often difficult to determine
whether "opposite" or "contrasting" items are contained in a sentence.
We would all probably agree that the words "hot" and "cold" are
antithetical, but is "marriage" antithetical to "tryst"? Is "back" the
opposite of "forth" in a sentence such as "Back and forth it went"?
Opinion may vary, and the discovery of antitheses in this study depends
on the judgment of the researcher. Aside from the problem of whether
an expression is or is not antithetical, however, there is no doubt that

many expressions are rather automatically antithetical, akin to the linguistically obligatory doublets. Thus, we have "sooner or later," "now or never," and "from dawn to dusk." None of these can be said truly to contain opposing ideas; they are simply ways of expressing time. Another type of seeming antithetical pairs is what might be called the "or not" antitheses, as in "whether or not" and "like it or not." Twenty-two writers of each group use antithesis, but again the range of the men's use is greater than that of the women. The range of the men's use is from one occurrence to twelve; the range for the women is one to nine. But there are also more men using antithesis more frequently: Rosten (12), Clark (8), Mander (7), Toffler (9), and Ellis (7), compared with FitzGerald (9) and Friday (7). The five male authors who use antithesis seven or more times account for 43 occurrences, or more than half of the 78 in their group; the two female authors who employ antithesis seven or more times account for 16 instances, or approximately one-quarter of the 65 instances in their group.

The impression that there is a predilection for antithesis among the males, despite a not much greater incidence in their overall sample, is reinforced by an examination of the antithetical statements of the "high" users. Such examination reveals that there are only three occurrences of the "automatic" variety, as when Ellis writes of bouncing "up and down." The two female "high users" likewise employ very few "automatic" antitheses: FitzGerald has none and Friday uses two—"more or less" and "begins and ends." Those writers of both sexes who employ much antithesis, therefore, do so consciously for rhetorical effect, and do not offer many cliché antitheses.

The antitheses, it should be noted, are contained within sentences; they do not signify a change in direction of argument (see Chapter 4) but simply offer opposing or contrasting ideas. And from the findings presented above, it does seem that men tend more than women to use antithesis for rhetorical effectiveness. The women's style in this respect might be said to be less contrastive than that of the men.

In summary, then, the 25 women writers of non-fiction employ more basic parallel constructions than do the men and a wider variety of co-occurring rhetorical devices of repetition. The differences in these aspects of style lie mainly in the kinds of rhetorical devices used by each group, with the men strongly preferring asyndeton over polysyndeton and the women balancing the two types. The men also prefer, although not so strongly, antithesis as an effective rhetorical device.

Fiction

One would expect, given the nature of the genre, that there is less parallelism in fiction than in non-fiction, and such is the case. Nonetheless, again excluding the totally unremarkable simple and complex doublets, the women fiction writers employ more parallelism than do the men fiction writers. The 25 women employ a total of 394 parallel constructions versus 321 used by the men, with greater use in both simple (183 to 159) and complex (211 to 162) constructions. A tabulation of the occurrence of the basic types of parallelism is given in Table 10.

Table 10. Basic Types of Parallelism: Fiction

Type	Instances in Men's Sample	Instances in Women's Sample
Simple doublet	71	89
Complex doublet	46	80
Simple triplet	59	61
Complex triplet	84	92
Simple series	29	33
Complex series	32	39

Whereas the women non-fiction writers use significantly more triplets than do the men, in the case of fiction the women use significantly more doublets. The men's two categories do not show this shift in type of parallelism. It would seem that the women accommodate to the genre of fiction by using the structurally simpler doublet instead of the triplet, although the doublets themselves are reinforced by one or more rhetorical devices.

With regard to the extended types of parallelism, that is, those basic types that are co-occurrent with at least one rhetorical device plus triplets and series without the devices of repetition, the women use 50 different parallelisms as compared with the men's use of 35. Thus, in fiction, as in non-fiction, the women's parallel structures are more varied because of higher use of and different combinations of the rhetorical devices. A summary of the comparative frequencies of rhetorical devices by the two groups is presented in Table 11.

Table 11. Frequency of Rhetorical Devices of Repetition: Fiction

Device	Instances in Men's Sample	Instances in Women's Sample
Polysyndeton	59	78
Asyndeton	59	80
Alliteration/ Homoioteleuton	30	42
Anaphora	52	66
Antithesis	31	42
Syllepsis	0	2
Tmesis	3	3
Epistrophe	5	6

The variation from the non-fiction style vis-à-vis polysyndeton and asyndeton resides in the men's fiction. The women fiction writers use both devices more often than do the men, as they did in the non-fiction sample, and they use the devices almost equally in fiction as in non-fiction. But the male writers use an equal number of asyndeta and polysyndeta in fiction, contrasting with their much more frequent use of asyndeta in non-fiction. The terseness conveyed by asyndeton is therefore found to be "masculine" in the non-fiction—but not in the fiction. Once again, the differences seem more marked in non-fiction, despite the stereotypes, which are based largely on fiction.

The incidence of polysyndeton in fiction is higher for both groups than it is in non-fiction, but the men use it 3.5 times more often in fiction, whereas the women use it only approximately ⅓ again as often in fiction. The device, however, does indicate less depth and complexity in sentence structure, as discussed previously; thus it seems only natural that it should occur more often in fiction. Of the 25 women fiction writers, 18 use polysyndeton; of the men fiction writers, 17 employ polysyndeton. The women's range of use is from one to 13 times per author, and the men's, from one to eight times. Nine of the women use polysyndeton four or more times: Didion (13), Newman (8), Uhnak and Block (7 each), MacDougall and Grau (6 each), Aiken (5), and Jaffe and Rhys (4 each). Seven men use it four or more times: O'Hara (8), Wicker and Vonnegut (7 each), Arnold and Burgess (6 each), Wallace (5), and Levey (4).

A few random examples from those of each group who use polysyndeton seven or more times serve to demonstrate that there is little difference in the tone established by the device:

Women:

She imagined her mother trying to call her from a pay phone . . . standing in a phone booth with all her quarters and dimes and nickels spread on the shelf and getting the operator and getting New York and then the answering service picking up the phone. (Joan Didion; *Play It As It Lays*)

The hand resting on his knee was pale and freckled and boneless and ever since he got in the car he had been humming "I Get a Kick Out of You." (Didion)

There's not going to be any money and there's not going to be any eating breakfast together and there's not going to be any getting married and there's not going to be any baby makes three. (Didion)

. . . when civilized talk and food and drink could be enjoyed . . . . (Andrea Newman; *The City Lover*)

They all looked curiously related to one another, all pretty and mousy and just under thirty, with headscarves and tweed coats and practical shoes. (Newman)

Her flesh was smooth and firm and rounded and her skin was startlingly white . . . . (Dorothy Uhnak; *Law and Order*)

. . . when he wanted to plunge and rip and devour . . . . (Uhnak)

Her incredible warmth and softness and fragrance and sweet fleshiness overwhelmed him. (Uhnak)

And wasn't it typical of what she'd gotten herself into that she estranged herself from everyone who was really close to her and the one she loved most was only partially hers and she didn't even have him near when she needed him most. (Jean Block; *Telfair's Daughter*)

He soothed her and comforted her and told her not to go to Greenwood . . . . (Block)

Men:

After a while the conversation settled down to a tempo: three or four mouthfuls of food, and some remark about movie extras and how some of them were easy to sleep with and some of them very difficult. (John O'Hara; *Hope of Heaven*)

He scratched a match and held it to the cigarette and cocked his head far over to one side and took a deep inhale. (O'Hara)

. . . here was where Lincoln sought to bind up a nation's wounds and Roosevelt dared fear itself and the bonus army marched to its sad, harsh fate. (Tom Wicker; *Facing the Lions*)

Morgan believed that spring . . . brought there as nowhere else its recurring, ignored reminder that something existed, something "flawless as truth and harsh as justice" functioned and repeated in nature, and had since long before man with his tools and his machines and his sciences began to shape and soften and restrain everything, began to make . . . . (Wicker)

The photographers milled and cursed and clicked in front of Hinman . . . . (Wicker)

He was a roaring furnace under all his layers of wool and straps and canvas. (Kurt Vonnegut; *Slaughterhouse Five*)

And then Weary tied in with two scouts, and they became close friends immediately, and they decided to fight their way back to their own lines. (Vonnegut)

He washed his cup and plate and knife and fork and spoon and saucepan . . . . (Vonnegut)

As can be seen, both the men and the women employ polysyndeton in simple and complex triplets and series, occasionally with anaphora or epistrophe. In most instances, there is an overtone of monotony, which may or may not extend to the entire sentence, depending upon the length of the polysyndetic structure and whether it is dominant in the sentence. The exception, perhaps, is Uhnak's use of polysyndeton, which is concerned throughout her sample almost entirely with sexual activity. Such activity does indeed often consist of repetitions and may even be monotonous; nonetheless, one suspects that Uhnak's purpose is not to convey monotony but rather to titillate.

As for asyndeton, the men use it as often in fiction as they do in non-fiction, whereas the women use it slightly less (88 occurrences in the women's non-fiction versus 80 in their fiction). Fewer men, however, employ it in fiction than in non-fiction (17 fiction authors and 20 non-fiction authors), whereas more women employ it in fiction than non-fiction (23 writers of fiction and 19 non-fiction authors). Of the 17 men, only five employ it four or more times in their samples: Wicker (10), Hegner (9), Longstreet (7), O'Hara (6), and Smith (4). Of the 23 women, 12 employ it four or more times: Didion and Newman (7 each), Oates (6), Alice Boyd, Ann Lorraine Thompson, and Jean Fairbairn (5 each) and Rona Jaffe, Martha Albrand, Dorothy Uhnak, Jeannie Sakol, Norma Meacock, and Jean Libman Block (4 each).

The range in this device is greater for the men, with Wicker's sample exhibiting 10 occurrences, but the average frequency of occurrence for the men and the women who do employ the device is exactly the same—just short of 3.5 occurrences per sample. Among the women, Didion and Newman can be termed "high" users of both polysyndeton and asyndeton. Among the men, only Wicker uses both polysyndeton and asyndeton seven or more times. But perhaps the most significant finding is that in fiction, the men and the women use both devices almost equally. In fiction, therefore, there is not the disparity between the two devices that exists in non-fiction. Both groups, in this regard, are "balanced."

In fiction there is diminished use by both groups of the other devices of repetition, with the exception of tmesis and epistrophe. Unlike the non-fiction writing, where other devices (except for antithesis) are employed equally by the men and the women, in fiction the women consistently use them more often. And with regard to antithesis, the women fiction writers reverse the ratio shown in non-fiction by using that particular device 25 percent more often than the male fiction writers do. Eighteen women fiction writers use antithesis; 14 men employ it. Only one author of either sex uses it as often as seven times—Charles Simmons—although two women's samples contain five instances each (Boyd and Sakol). Almost all instances of antithesis, however, consist of the automatic, cliché variety, with a plethora of "up and down"s, "before and after"s, "sooner or later"s, "on and off"s, and "back and forth"s. Two of Simmons' antitheses are of this variety, as well as two of Boyd's and one of Sakol's. It is thus questionable how meaningful a device antithesis is in fiction.

Summary

The women writers of both non-fiction and fiction employ the basic types of parallelism more often than do the men writers and in more varied ways. Their use of the rhetorical devices of repetition is also more frequent and varied, although the differences between the men's and women's writing is considerably more marked in non-fiction than in fiction. In general, the women are more even-handed in their use of the devices than are the men; they do not go to the extremes of asyndeton and polysyndeton that characterize the men's writing.

It is apparent that the women are not "unbalanced." If anything, they are more balanced than the men. Likewise, they are as a group more aware of rhetoric than the men; they are more aware of effect than the men. And yet, because of the balanced nature of their writing, their style in this respect can be termed conservative, or "middle of the road."

Chapter 6

The "Masculine" Simile and the "Feminine" Simile

Chief among those stylistic devices that express figurative or imaginative perceptions are, of course, the metaphor and the simile. The metaphor, however, is a slippery thing, difficult to define formally. We can agree, for example, that such a commonplace statement as "The road is a ribbon" is indeed a metaphor, but we are also faced with elusive metaphorical expressions such as "He was deep in grief," or "Her heart was high," or "He was covered with guilt," or "Jim is a real prince," all of which are also very commonplace but rarely recognized as metaphorical expressions. The root of the problem is simply that most metaphors so pervade our language as to be linguistic rather than stylistic matters.

To some degree, the same problem exists with regard to the simile. But the simile is more clearly defined in terms of structure, for all similes are comparisons involving the use of the words "like" or "as." Even though similes are usually considered the "weaker" of the two devices because they suggest comparison rather than identity, they are not "buried" in the language and are easier to recognize than metaphors simply because they do involve the intervening words.

To define the simile in terms of *meaning,* the main rule of thumb is that the person or object being compared to something else is in fact *not* the same as the "something else." Marilyn Monroe "as a sex symbol," for example, is not regarded as a simile, for she is (or was) a sex symbol, but Hitler "as a fish out of water" is regarded as a simile, albeit scarcely a startling one.

The simile can thus be very commonplace. But commonplace or not, it is a reliable measure of style in terms of imaginative expression, with the use of striking or original similes indicating a higher quality of imagination than the use of commonplace similes. A study of the similes occurring in the writing of the men and the women might be expected to reveal differences in the quality of imagination and perception, as well as whether the women are less imaginative (more "insipid") than the men.

Nonetheless, in the prose of the two groups, there is little quantitative difference in the use of similes in fiction. In non-fiction, the women use half again as many similes as the men—50 occurrences in the women's writing versus 35 in the men's non-fiction. The generally low incidence of the simile in non-fiction, however, vitiates against claiming a marked difference between the two groups. And as can be expected, there are many more similes employed by both groups of fiction writers: 75 instances by the women and 69 by the men.

Non-Fiction

Of the 25 male non-fiction writers, 15 employ at least one simile, with a range up to six occurrences. Fifteen women also employ at least one simile, with a range up to seven occurrences. A frequency distribution of the simile in the non-fiction authors is given in Table 12.

Although there is perceptible quantitative difference between the two groups, a study of those authors who use the simile four or more times does not reveal much qualitative difference. Such differences may exist among individual writers.

Among the men, Hunter Thompson's similes can by no means be termed commonplace. Writing of the 1972 Presidential campaign, he sees Hubert Humphrey as "a treacherous brain-damaged old vulture," the Muskie "nightmare" as a "political watershed," the Muskie delegates as "the rancid cream of the party." He likens three weeks in Washington to "three years in a mineshaft underneath Butte, Montana," and finds the idea of Ted Kennedy running for Vice-President

Table 12. Frequency Distribution of Similes: Non-Fiction

Men		Women	
Author	Number of Occurrences	Author	Number of Occurrences
Thompson	6	Lindbergh	7
Mailer	5	Maynard	6
Goodavage	4	Friday	6
Greene	4	Chesler	5
Langer	3	DeMille	4
Peter	3	Houston	4
Toffler	2	Steiner	4
Belz	1	Cartland	3
Bing	1	Farmer	3
Carey	1	Brothers	2
Ellis	1	Vilar	2
Maas	1	Cohen	1
Pilat	1	Fisher	1
Rovere	1	Gordon	1
Salisbury	1	Holmes	1

akin to "the Jets trading Joe Namath to the Dallas Cowboys as a sub for Roger Staubach." His largely hostile political commentary is often funny, whether one agrees with his opinions or not. Thus, for Thompson, the simile is an instrument of wit.

Mailer's similes are quite different from those of Thompson, for he is writing about the moon-shot and attempting to describe both visually and viscerally the contrasts of space involved in that project. An astronaut is, for example, likened to a "particle of dust"; outer space is like "a house with no walls and no ceiling"; the two spacecraft are attached "like the most unhappy version of Siamese twins"; and solar flares are like "a great cloth or broom."

There is some similarity in Goodavage's use of similes, probably because of subject matter, for Goodavage is writing about a comet. An eclipse is described as "a great curtain pulled over the sky"; comets float as if "attached to invisible parachutes"; and systems of constellations are compared to "strings of lights on a Christmas tree."

Greene's similes might be described as emotional (in the sense that they convey a particular emotional response), as well as visual. They are not at all humorous. He talks, for instance, of pulling a trigger as casually as "taking an aspirin tablet"; of walking down a road that is "smooth and shiny like the walls of a public lavatory"; of time moving as slowly as "the unemployed bands of those days"; and of a sense of jubilation as if "carnival lights had been switched on in a dark drab street."

The similes of the four men are distinctive and original; there are no clichés. Most of the similes used by the other men—and less often than four times—are banal: "pillar of the Church," "fish out of water," and "breath of fresh air" are typical.

Among the women non-fiction writers who use the simile comparatively often, we find that Lindbergh's are largely visual and occasionally expressive of emotion or particular feelings. Thus, asparagus stalks are compared to "icicles," islands are compared to "little boats in a harbor," the Breadwater is compared to "a straight flagpole," and the coast, peninsula, bay, etc., are "flowing as though swept in a great wind out to sea." But Lindbergh also speaks of publicity as like "being born without a nose," and the look indicating recognition as akin to watching "a public amusement, monkeys in a cage."

There is not so strong a visual quality in Maynard's similes, although she does describe sperm as "tadpoles." But she also compares a television show to "a yeastless dough," the Donna Reed Show to "pleasant grade-B detective stories," and going to Church to "going to Brownies," all indicating negative responses to what is being described, although without the evident hostility or wit that is found in Hunter Thompson's similes.

Friday, in her book on women's sexual fantasies, uses exclusively non-visual comparisons. She likens the themes and devices of sexual fantasy to the leitmotifs of the "toad prince and moustached villain of fairy tales"; encouragement is like "the occasional flick a child gives to a spinning top"; and trying to convey the emotion, meaning, and experience of sexual fantasy through euphemism is similar to "giving a thirsty man a piece of paper with the word 'water' written on it." There is no particular feeling discernible in her smiles; rather, they convey ideas.

Chesler's similes are likewise non-visual and are often negative (cf. Thompson and Maynard). She finds that clinicians are like "ghetto schoolteachers," that the role of women in public institutions is a form of "dying colonialism," and that women's sexuality is considered an "act of incest." The negative quality, however, is not hostility but rather anger at what she regards as mistaken concepts.

Of the three other women writers who use four or more similes, only Steiner's exhibit her feelings. In her book dealing with her relationship with Sylvia Plath, she says, when talking of their friendship, "we wore each other like a pair of matching talismans." Later, however, she feels that she (Steiner) was being cast as "Judas in a passion play," and that her encounters with Plath were like "the clash of opposing cultures."

Houston's film criticism includes descriptions of characters in an Italian film as "Renaissance princes," film-makers as "boxers," and cinematic effects as "pulling at a piece of elastic." DeMille's autobiography contains the most commonplace of the similes in this group. Ramon is seen as "a bridgegroom," the city as "a dynamo," and naked girls swimming in patterns as "a starfish."

With the exception of the similes of Thompson, however, and possibly Chesler, there seems to be little difference in the quality of the men's and women's similes as distinct groups. They all range from the visual to the visceral (or emotional) to the "ideational." But the women do use similes more often than the men in non-fiction. They do, therefore, perceive persons, sights, and ideas in terms of other sets of persons, sights, and ideas more often than do the men. The women cannot be termed unimaginative.

Fiction

If there is some quantitative but not qualitative difference between the similes of the men and the women in non-fiction, the opposite seems to obtain in fiction. In the fiction category, 21 of the 25 women's samples contain from one to nine similes, for a total of 77 occurrences. Twenty-four of the 25 men's samples contain from one to ten similes, for a total of 69. Neither the range nor the number is very different between the two groups. Ten of the men use only one simile, however, whereas only

Table 13. Frequency Distribution of Similes: Fiction

Men		Women	
Author	Number of Occurrences	Author	Number of Occurrences
MacDonald	10	Oates	9
Breen	9	Aiken	8
Longstreet	7	Shulman	7
Sheed	6	Albrand	6
Brown	5	Gould	6
Houston	4	Buchanan	4
Alpert	3	Drexler	4
Hegner	3	DuMaurier	4
Levey	2	Meacock	4
Malamud	2	Rhys	4
Smith	2	Block	3
Vonnegut	2	Boyd	3
Wallace	2	Newman	3
Wicker	2	Grau	2
Arnold	1	Mitford	2
Burgess	1	Renault	2
Carlino	1	Sakol	2
Gilbert	1	Didion	1
Kazan	1	Fairbairn	1
Kemelman	1	Holt	1
O'Hara	1	Jaffe	1
Roth	1		
Simmons	1		
Stewart	1		

four of the women use only one. Among the 24 men, therefore, they either use the simile rather frequently or very infrequently (cf. the men's use of exclamation points), and the 21 women use it more evenly. A frequency distribution of similes in fiction is presented in Table 13.

There is a striking divergence, however, in the similes that apply to men or women. The similes used by the women writers applied to men and women connote vastly different perceptions of themselves and of

Table 14. Similes in Women's Fiction

Author	Simile
As Applied to a Woman or to Women	
Shulman	"a has-been like last year's Miss America"
Drexler	"a stray piece of meat"
Oates	"women on movie posters"
	"a terrible blow"–"the danger of women"
Newman	"a man on a health farm"–i.e., starving
Meacock	"a stone"
Gould	"wisps of silver like drifting mist"
Buchanan	"a part of the garden"
Aiken	"stuffed dummies"
Block	"a proud young colt"
	"the passion flower"
As applied to a Man or to Men	
Renault	"ravens to share the spoils"
Aiken	"Lippizaner on a milk-round"
Buchanan	"monster"
Drexler	"chameleon"
Albrand	"monkey"
Sakol	"raisins in the cake"
	"prelate at an orgy"
DuMaurier	"unweaned lambs"
	"pouter-pigeon"

men from those perceptions of the men writers as expressed in their similes concerning men and women. Similes are, of course, not the only manner in which such perceptions can be indicated, but at least they furnish highly useful clues. Exemplification of such differences is contained in Table 14.

The women's views of both themselves and men indicate a fair degree of ambivalence. With regard to themselves, the similes range from highly self-denigrative ("a has-been," "a stray piece of meat") to vaguely threatening (Oates' only: "women on movie posters" are seen as dangerously seductive; "the danger of women" is "a terrible blow") to utterly passive ("a stone," "stuffed dummies") to romantic ("wisps of silver," "proud young colt," "the passion flower"). Their perceptions of men are more polarized. Men, likened most often to some form of animal, are seen as either untrustworthy and rapacious or as incompetent, pretentious fools. They are "ravens," "monsters," "chameleons"— or they are "monkeys," "prelates at an orgy," "unweaned lambs," "pouter-pigeons." The only simile expressing any sort of admiration is the "Lippizaner on a milk-round," a noble animal forced to do ignoble work. The "raisins in the cake" simile, where men are portrayed as the goodies to be devoured by a woman, is not unlike the view of men as incompetent fools, although the implied aggressiveness of the woman is much stronger than in the other similes.

Three of the women writers offer similes for both men and women: Aiken, Drexler, and Buchanan. Where Aiken's women are stuffed dummies, her man is a highly trained and highly bred horse; Drexler's woman is only a "stray piece of meat" and her man is an untrustworthy "chameleon"; Buchanan sees a woman as a "part of the garden"—rather vapidly floral—but her man is a "monster." The three women who offer similes for both sexes thus seem to typify the range of perceptions regarding women and men characteristic of all the women writers.

In general, however, the women are confused about their perceptions of themselves and contradictory about their perceptions of men. For if they picture men as "monkeys" and "raisins in the cake," they imply that women are superior, dominant, and controlling, and the men are to be derided. If, on the other hand, men are perceived as "ravens" and "monsters," the women, by implication, are powerless victims. The women as a group hold both views of men.

An examination of the men's similes for themselves and women indicates quite different perceptions (see Table 15).

Table 15. Similes in Men's Fiction

Author	Simile
As Applied to a Woman or to Women	
MacDonald	"buxom angels"
Wallace	"a Marie Laurencin picture"
Longstreet	"an arpeggio of violins"
Simmons	"an apple"
Houston	"a young girl" (the woman is not a young girl in fact)
Alpert	"a child"
Kazan	"a child"
Levey	"an attentive child"
Brown	"a small child"
As Applied to a Man or to Men	
Brown	"an aging gorilla"
	"a personal secretary" (the man is a native gun-bearer in fact)
Longstreet	"a hovering ghost"
	"a roan horse"
Carlino	"a cat"
Hegner	"a dog"
Gilbert	(not) "a swine"
Smith	"a great bear"
	"a lizard"
Houston	"an old man" (the man is not an old man in fact)
Breen	"a wild cat"

There is not one threatening image in the men's similes concerning women. Quite the contrary, the men unanimously view women as innocent, as ethereal, and, most insistently, as children. The lack of any adult imagery is striking. (Conversely, the women *never* regard men as children.) There is certainly no ambivalence or contradiction on the part of the men when they use similes for women. The woman-as-failed-adult is a pervasive perception. Thus, as far as the men are concerned, they—the men—are totally dominant, superior, realistic, and mature. The woman is consistently diminished.

The men's similes for men are also consistent, in that, with the exception of Breen's "a wild cat," there is nowhere a simile implying danger or threat. (Smith's "a great bear" is, in context, a friendly bear.) Instead, we have cats, dogs, horses (the "roan horse," for some reason, is equated with health), and aging (impotent) gorillas and men. The men, therefore, see themselves as harmless animals or presences, and neither as untrustworthy "swine" nor as any sort of monsters.

Breen, as mentioned, offers the one exception, but it is an exception that within his own sample is entirely consistent, for he writes of a man's hair as "a black flag," a man's legs as "murderous pistons," a man's teeth as those of a "skeleton." Further, when he refers to a character's "smiling like an angel," the context indicates that there is deceit involved in the smile. Breen seems to be dealing solely with the male-as-sadist, one of the views held by the women.

Houston, Brown, and Longstreet offer similes for both sexes. Houston's "young girl" is matched by his "old man"—a rather limited range, one might say. Brown's "small child" is matched by his "aging gorilla"; and Longstreet's "arpeggio of violins" is paired with his "hovering ghost." The three men, in other words, encompass the stereotypical views of women and men commented on above.

The only area, with regard to these types of similes, in which the men and women agree is in the preponderant animal terminology applied to men. Neither group, with the exception of Block's "proud young colt," describes women in terms of animals. But it is clear that the animal terminology as employed by the men has vastly different connotations from that used by the women.

Generally speaking, then, the male fiction writers regard women as children and themselves as harmless creatures. Their view of women and of themselves, as contrasted with the women's view, is quite consistent and unambiguous.

There is probably something to be said for a simplistic view of humankind—but not much. The men's persistent implication that they themselves are kindly, well-meaning creatures and that the women have not grown up is a pleasant fiction for them to maintain. Such a view supports a complacent conviction of superiority.

People and people's perceptions of people, however, are not simple; to aver that they are flies in the face of fact. A simplistic view on the part of the men, therefore, might quite possibly be a form of defense— defense against dealing with the confusion and unpredictability and hostility and damage that make up a great part of life. Actually, in a curious way, it makes little sense (even as a defense) for the men to see women as children *and* themselves as harmless creatures—in other words, to see both sexes as harmless. For the will to perceive women as children is also the will *not* to see women as women, and the will to see men as non-threatening creatures is also the will *not* to see men as men. To describe the men *and* the women as helpless and dependent is a form of whistling in the dark, of refusing to risk the "dangers" of women as mature people. If, therefore, there is an underlying anxiety in the men's persistent view of women as children, if they are, as it were, trying to sell themselves on this view rather than believing it to be true, then they are carefully hedging their bets in their descriptions of themselves. For the woman-as-child perception does not create a "need" for the man-as-kindly-creature. Woman-as-danger would create a need for such protective coloration.

In all, there seems to be a kind of denial of reality in the men's similes regarding men and women. And a denial of reality can be both consoling and comforting.

The "uncomfortable" views are those adopted by the women. They are confused; they do not see themselves *or* men in any consistent manner. But their similes do reveal that the women perceive both men and women in both positive and negative ways; both men and women are perceived as predators and victims, as innocent and evil, as frightening and reassuring. It is suggested, therefore, that the women, in their fiction similes, are closer to portraying the confusion and contradiction that inhere in all people's perceptions.

Summary

In non-fiction, the women writers employ more similes than do the men, but there is no discernible qualitative difference between those in one group and those in the other. There are individual differences and similarities among the non-fiction writers as a whole, however.

The use of similes in fiction is another matter. The two groups employ almost the same number of similes, but there is strong divergence in those similes describing men and those describing women as used by each group. The men's similes depicting both men and women are largely consistent, but are simplistic in nature, with women being compared most often to children. This somewhat unrealistic view is not found in the women's similes describing men and women, where the views are ambivalent and conflicting. These views, because of their complexity and inconsistency, are considered to be more honestly representative of the nature of people's perceptions than those of the men.

In neither fiction nor non-fiction can the women writers be termed "unimaginative" in the use of similes. The quantity is greater in their non-fiction, and their range is greater in fiction.

Chapter 7

Who Really Uses More Adverbs?

There exists a belief that women's speech is characterized—or caricatured—by "gushiness," and the most commonly cited symptom of such gushiness is what is thought to be women's excessive use of adverbs, particularly those modifying adjectives. The linguist Otto Jespersen states that women have a "fondness for hyperbole," which leads them to use many "adverbs of intensity . . . very often with disregard of their proper meaning."[1] Jespersen, however, does not back his statement with objective findings. Thus it is only a matter of his opinion or belief. Because he is a noted linguist, however, his beliefs take on the quality of authority, particularly since they coincide with stereotyped notions of women's speech. It is women who are reputed to overuse the hyperbolic adverb, as in "utterly divine," "simply great," etc.

Whether this belief about women's speech is erroneous is not at issue in this study unless women's speech patterns carry over into their writing styles. On the assumption that at least to a certain extent they do, the prediction would be that women employ more adverbs than men in their writing—*if* Jespersen is correct.

Doubts have already been cast on his statements, however, notably by Kramer, who reports finding no significant difference in the frequency of use of adverbs in written composition by two small groups of men and women college students.[2] The present study concerning professional men and women writers confirms Kramer's numerical findings but indicates that there are other differences between the two groups.

The adverbs under consideration are only the so-called *-ly* adverbs, obviously those ending in *-ly,* since these are the ones chiefly involved in hyperbolic use. In the men's non-fiction sample of 50,000 words, there are 640 *-ly* adverbs; the women's non-fiction sample contains 577. Thus, in non-fiction, the men actually use more adverbs than the women. In fiction, the ratio is reversed. The men use 528 adverbs versus the women's 605. In the combined fiction and non-fiction by women (100,000 words), the women use 529 *different* adverbs (called "types") and use them a total of 1182 times (each instance called a "token"), whereas the men's combined fiction and non-fiction contains 509 different adverbs used a total of 1158 times. The "type/token ratios" of the two groups are therefore almost precisely the same: .447 for the women and .439 for the men. In terms of numbers and frequencies, once again we find there is practically no difference between the two groups—that, based on the occurrence of *-ly* adverbs, the women are not "gushier" than the men.

In non-fiction, there is some difference in the range of frequency among the authors of each group. The men's writing contains from two (Toffler) to 70 (Ellis) adverbs, whereas the women's non-fiction ranges from six (Gordon) to 43 (Steiner) adverbs.

In fiction, there is likewise some difference in the range of adverb usage, but in the reverse direction from that of non-fiction. The men's fiction contains from seven (Longstreet) to 38 (Brown) adverbs; the women's fiction contains from six (Renault) to 45 (Boyd) adverbs. But, although the range of the women's use of adverbs is slightly higher than that in the men's fiction (39 to 29), it is still nowhere near so high as that of the men's non-fiction, where the range is 68.

Also, the range of the women's adverb use in fiction and non-fiction is almost the same (37 in non-fiction, 39 in fiction), whereas the men's range of adverb use drops sharply from 68 in non-fiction to 29 in fiction. The women's use of adverbs is more consistent and less extreme than that of the men.

Modification Patterns

How the adverbs are used, or what they modify, reveals some difference between the two groups. Three types of modification are investigated: verbs, adjectives, and constructions. (The latter are those most often occurring at the beginning or end of sentences or clauses, traditionally considered verbal modifiers. Modern linguists, however, feel that such use actually indicates modification of an entire construction.) A tabulation of the findings is shown in Table 16.

Table 16. Modification by Adverbs

	Verbs	Adjectives	Constructions
Non-fiction			
Men	70%	21%	8%
Women	71%	23%	4%
Fiction			
Men	78%	15%	6%
Women	72%	21%	4%

In non-fiction, it is clear that there is little difference in the types of modification used by the men and the women. In fiction, however, the men's use of the adverbs to modify verbs rises and their use to modify adjectives drops proportionately. The women, on the other hand, do not use a pattern of modification in their fiction that is markedly different from their non-fiction.

In this way also, therefore, there is a consistency in the women's writing that is not found in the men's prose. The drop in the total number of adverbs in the men's fiction as compared to their non-fiction, the comparative drop in range between the two categories, and the drop in the use of adjectival modification in fiction, coupled with the rise of verbal modification, all add up to the non-qualified type of writing that exists in their fiction, but not in their non-fiction. These findings suggest an uncompromising "macho" quality in their fiction that does not reside in their non-fiction. They also suggest that the women's fiction and non-fiction styles do not differ markedly in terms of adverb usage.

"Simply"

The adverb "simply" is often attributed to women's speech, especially as an adjectival modifier. But the fact of the matter is that, in the non-fiction of both groups, it is used more often by the men than by the women. Fourteen men use "simply" a total of 20 times, never more than twice per author, and eleven women use it 13 times, again never more than twice. Furthermore, the word is used to modify an adjective only once by a man and once by a woman:

> . . . simply 'unusual' clouds . . . (Goodavage)

> . . . it was, simply, impossible . . . (Hodge)

One might expect that the use of "simply" would increase in the fiction sample because of the greater proportion of dialogue presumably reflecting speech patterns. Such, however, is not the case. Both the men and the women use the adverb less frequently in fiction. Four women use it a total of five times; four men use it a total of four times. Only one woman writer uses it to modify an adjective, perhaps hyperbolically:

> . . . it was simply horrible . . . .(Mitford)

One man uses "simply" in an utterance ascribed to a female character:

> I'm simply dying for uncomplicated companionship. (Alpert)

The latter example is distinctly hyperbolic, but it is only attributed to a woman speaker, not written by a woman writer.

"Utterly" and "Awfully"

The adverb "utterly," contrary to belief, is used rarely by either men or women in either fiction or non-fiction. In non-fiction, Goodavage uses "utterly terrifying"; Lindbergh writes "utterly apart from flying" and "utterly bitter about it." In fiction, Hegner writes "utterly insatiable," and Aiken writes "utterly at a loss." With "utterly" occurring only five times in 200,000 words of prose, there would seem to be utterly no basis for the belief in the pervasiveness of such an hyperbolic adverb in women's language.

The adverb "awfully," also frequently thought of as a feminine intensifier, as in "That's awfully nice of you," is used only by the men, with one occurrence in their non-fiction and one in their fiction.

Men's Adverbs and Women's Adverbs

There are, nonetheless, certain adverbs that only the men use and certain others that only the women use. If we examine the non-fiction first, we find that only the men (and no women) use the following adverbs three or more times:

> consequently (4)
> exactly (5)
> strictly (3)
> surely (5)
> wryly (3)

We also find that only the women (and no men) use the following adverbs three or more times:

> cheerfully (3)
> desperately (4)
> scarcely (3)

That there is some difference in the nature of the two groups, in terms of emotionality, is evident even in non-fiction, but this matter is discussed more fully subsequently.

In fiction, there are also different sets of adverbs used solely by the men or solely by the women, although certain ones may or may not occur less frequently in non-fiction. Only in the men's fiction (and not at all in the women's) do we find the following adverbs occurring three or more times:

> abruptly (6)

> seriously (3)
> silently (5)

whereas the following adverbs occur three or more times only in the women's fiction:

> deeply (4)
> endlessly (3)
> faintly (3)
> perfectly (5)
> positively (3)
> wildly (4)

There would seem to be a considerable difference in the quality of the men's and women's adverbs that overrides the difference between the categories of fiction and non-fiction. The adverbs used solely by the men in each category are basically unemotional as compared with those by the women in each category. Those "fiction-men-only" adverbs may occur in the non-fiction of either group, however; for example, "abruptly" does occur twice in the non-fiction by the women. Likewise, a "non-fiction-women-only" adverb may occur in the fiction of either men or women, as, for example, the adverb "scarcely," which does occur once in both the men's and the women's fiction.

Thus a fairer test of whether there is a qualitative difference between the exclusively male adverbs and the exclusively female adverbs would be to consider the adverbs as they occur in fiction and non-fiction combined. If we do so, we find that in 200,000 words of prose, men and only men use the following adverbs three or more times:

> casually (4)
> stiffly (3)
> thickly (4)

Furthermore, women and only women use the following adverbs:

> bravely (3)
> cheerfully (4)
> desperately (6)
> painfully (3)

> positively (5)
> self-consciously (3)
> unexpectedly (3)
> unwittingly (3)
> wildly (5)

It is abundantly clear that the men-only adverbs as they occur in the entire study are far more detached and unemotional than those of the women. By contrast, the women's adverbs are highly emotional, laden with a sense of effort. With the possible exception of "positively," there is nothing even remotely detached about them, and even the manner in which "positively" is used by the women most often reveals strong feeling:

> *positively un-American* (LeShan)

> *The Morris Cohen on Wall Street positively confirmed that my mother had lived* . . . . (Fisher)

> . . . *the Sudetanland was positively Hitler's last territorial demand* . . . . (Mitford)

> *positively dowdy* . . . . (Shulman)

> *the village* . . . *seemed* . . . *a positively lunar distance.* (Newman)

Only Fisher's use of the adverb is factual; the others, in which the adverb modifies an adjective, are strongly emotional intensifiers.

The women-only adverbs throughout the entire study would thus seem to be the polar opposites of the men-only adverbs in terms of emotionality.

Adverbs of Emotion and Adverbs of Pace

This kind of difference suggests a basis for the frequently expressed critical opinion that women write in an "emotional" style and logically leads to an investigation of *all* the adverbs of emotion or "state of mind" occurring in the 200,000-word sample. Such adverbs include words like "abjectly," "aggressively," "amiably," "angrily," "bitterly," "coldly," and so on through the alphabet. The findings bear out the emotional quality of the women-only adverbs discussed above, but *only* with regard to fiction. A tabulation of results is shown in Table 17.

Table 17. Adverbs of Emotion

	Non-fiction	Fiction
Men	34	23
Women	34	49

With the men and women using the same number of adverbs of emotion in their non-fiction, we can see that with regard to adverb usage, the main differences occur in fiction. As mentioned earlier, the men use fewer adverbs in their fiction than in their non-fiction, covering a narrower range of frequency, and fewer adverbs modifying adjectives. They also use fewer adverbs of emotion in their fiction. Although the women's use of adverbs in fiction and non-fiction is not so differentiated as is the men's in terms of modification and range, their use of the adverbs of emotion increases in fiction in almost precisely the same ratio as they decrease in the men's fiction.

Among the adverbs of emotion, there are, as with the other adverbs in general, those used only by men and those used only by women in addition to those already discussed (all of which occur three or more times). The men's non-fiction, for example, contains the only instances of "angrily," "consciously," and "romantically," each occurring twice. There are no instances of women's adverbs used only in non-fiction occurring more than once, but those that are found once include "abjectly," "confidently," "ecstatically," "embarrassingly," "gloomily," and "reluctantly."

In fiction, only the women's writing contains "amiably," "gaily," and "miserably," twice in each case. "Coolly" is found only in the men's fiction, and it occurs twice.

Thus, the men's total use of adverbs of emotion is lower than that of the women (57 instances versus 83), and their emotions differ from the women's qualitatively as well. Only the men, it can be said, are angry, romantic, or cool, whereas only the women are abject, gloomy, miserable *or* gay, ecstatic, or confident. The note of depression in the women's adverbs, counterbalanced by cheeriness, is simply not found in the men's adverbs of emotion.

If, however, there seems to be evidence that the women are more "emotional" than the men, insofar as their fiction style is concerned, is it also true that the men's style is more "active"? If, in other words, the women tend to be more concerned with the nature of their feelings, are the men more concerned with the nature of their actions? These questions led to an investigation of the adverbs of pace or timing, comprising the adverbs of "pace" listed in Table 18, and the instances by men and women in both fiction and non-fiction.

Table 18. Adverbs of Pace

Adverb	Instances in Non-fiction		Instances in Fiction	
	Men	Women	Men	Women
abruptly	0	2	6	0
gradually	7	1	3	4
hastily	1	1	1	1
hurriedly	0	0	0	1
immediately	5	5	17	6
quickly	6	8	13	6
rapidly	2	2	5	1
slowly	5	8	24	17
suddenly	6	8	17	13
swiftly	0	0	0	1
Totals	32	35	86	50

Once again, it can be seen that the differences between the two groups reside in their fiction rather than their non-fiction. The men's fiction contains approximately 70 percent more adverbs of pace than the women's. There is an apparent active quality to the men's fiction as opposed to the emotive quality of the women's.

Nonetheless, it should be pointed out that the women's fiction is, in terms of the two types of adverbs ("emotion" and "pace"), far more balanced than is that of the men. The women's fiction contains almost exactly the same number of adverbs of emotion (49) and adverbs of pace (50). The men's fiction, on the other hand, contains almost four times as many adverbs of pace as adverbs of emotion: 86 of pace and 23 of emotion.

It can be said that the women have once again chosen a middle-of-the-road mode of expression. And with their fiction containing a like number of the two types of adverbs, it cannot be said that their fiction is excessively "emotional," for they are apparently as concerned with the quality of action as with the quality of emotion. It is rather the men whose fiction seems disproportionately concerned with the quality of action and a lack of concern with the quality of feeling. The men writers of fiction can therefore be characterized as *lacking* in emotion in the context of the evenly balanced nature of the women's fiction.

The women's fiction style in this respect is also once again closer to their non-fiction style than are the men's styles in the two categories. The women's use of adverbs of emotion in their fiction increases by 15 occurrences; their use of adverbs of pace in their fiction increases by precisely the same amount. The men's use of adverbs of pace increases in their fiction by 54, so that their use of these two types of adverbs in fiction and non-fiction diverges by 65 occurrences in opposite directions.

The study of the occurrences of one "neutral" adverb—i.e., concerned with neither emotion nor pace—offers support for the observation that the women's fiction and non-fiction styles do not differ so sharply as do those of the men. The adverb "probably" is used 20 times in men's non-fiction and only eight times in their fiction. "Probably" occurs in the women's non-fiction 12 times, and in their fiction 13 times. If the word itself connotes a lack of certainty, a hedging of the bets, then it is clear that the men are far less willing to be equivocal in their fiction than in their non-fiction, whereas the women's use of "probably" does not vary. The avoidance of a flat statement by the use of the particular adverb is called for in careful writing. But the men's caution in their non-fiction is severely curtailed in their fiction; they *must* sound positive in their fiction.

"Really"

There is one more specific adverb that must be considered because the women use it far more often than the men. This is the adverb "really." In non-fiction, 15 women use it for a total of 26 times; six men use it for a total of nine times. This is such a striking difference that some exemplification might indicate how—or possibly why—this adverb is used so much more often by the women:

Women's Use of "Really"—Non-fiction:

Cohen (4)

> . . . *passivity in women is really fatigue.*

> . . . *if they'd really tried . . . .*

> . . . *husband doesn't really care . . . .*

> . . . *I really can't offer any advice . . . .*

Maynard (4)

> *I could not really take . . . .*

> . . . *she really needed them . . . .*

> . . . *felt really graceful . . . .*

> . . . *what's really going on . . . .*

LeShan (3)

I'm really not horrified . . . .

. . . we don't really want . . . .

. . . there is really no earthly reason . . . .

Brothers (2)

. . . a man who can really use this education . . . .

. . . a man who could really benefit . . . .

Cartland (2)

. . . feelings did not really matter . . . .

She looked really beautiful . . . .

Sanders (2)

I really could have gotten . . . .

. . . we really understand all her ways . . . .

DeMille (1)

Are you really going to Ramon?

Fisher (1)

. . . that really doesn't concern your husband . . . .

Friday (1)

. . . we really love one another . . . .

Holmes (1)

I really don't want very much . . . .

Howar (1)

It really did not matter . . . .

Lindbergh (1)

C. cãn really make it go . . . .

Schreiber (1)

. . . it was really a partition . . . .

Vilar (1)

. . . things that really matter . . . .

Men's Use of "Really"—Non-fiction:

Ellis (2)

. . . he and his mate really want . . . .

. . . mammaries are really sweat glands . . . .

Maas (2)

No I really mean it.

. . . what they really want . . . .

Mankiewicz (2)

Truth was never really an option.

. . . the question, really, must have been . . . .

Peter (1)

. . . no longer is really a destination . . . .

Rovere (1)

. . . where the exploiting is really good . . . .

Smith (1)

. . . the really active opposition . . . .

Except in certain instances, the use of "really" carries a note of doubt, doubt that the audience/reader will accept a statement, not doubt on the part of the speaker/writer. It is the doubt of the speaker/writer with respect to the audience that leads to the presumed reinforcing use of the adverb. Something is "really," truly, honestly, factually so. But the very occurrence of the adverb suggests doubt on the part of the speaker/writer that may or may not be accurate. In other words, when, for example, Cartland says "feelings did not really matter," one wonders if Cartland herself does not entertain doubts. This note of doubt camouflaged by the use of "really" occurs in the men's use of the adverb too, notably in the first five instances cited.

Among those instances where "really" does not imply doubt are Schreiber's, Ellis' second example, and probably Rovere's and Smith's.

It should be noted that only the women seem concerned with what "really" does or does not "matter," although both groups "really"do or do not "want" in equal proportion.

As for the frequency of "really" in fiction, again the women use the adverb more frequently than the men. Fourteen women use the word 33 times; twelve men use it 25 times. The disparity is not so great as in non-fiction, although, as in the use of other adverbs, the frequency of the women's use in fiction and non-fiction is much closer than the frequency of use by the men in the two categories. In other words, in this particular respect, the men's fiction and non-fiction repeat the sharply divergent pattern observed in other usages, whereas the usage in the women's fiction is not vastly different from their usage in non-fiction.

However, in examining only the fiction of both groups, where the women use "really" only 25 percent more often than the men, certain instances and contexts indicate that women in general are *perceived* by both the men and the women to use "really" excessively. The women's use ranges from one to six occurrences per author, with Jean Rhys employing it most frequently. Her sample deserves scrutiny:

> *Do I really look like . . . .*

> *. . . something really funny . . . .*

> *. . . what do you really like worse . . . .*

> *"Really, really, really"—that's all you can say!*

The last example is the utterance of a male character who is mocking the female narrator's manner of speaking.

The men's range in fiction is from 1 to 10 occurrences (Burgess). However, scattered throughout the men's fiction are three instances attributed to the speech of female characters:

> *. . . they're really here!* (Higgins)

> *I really don't know . . . .* (Levey)

> *I really don't know . . . .* (MacDonald)

There is thus some indication on the part of both the men and women writers that women use "really" more often.

The striking exception to the pattern is Anthony Burgess, who employs "really" far more often than any woman writer, yet whose novel is a first person narrative by a man:

. . . a show which Howard said was really depressing . . . .

. . . rather pretty and funny really . . . .

. . . what really can you do with money . . . .

. . . that week I was really sick.

. . . more like a joint really . . . .

dash to the bathroom to be really sick.

. . . it was really amazing . . . .

. . . some really very strong coffee . . . .

. . . I found him very nice too, and really charming . . . .

And, really, it wasn't a very interesting show.

It can be argued that, because Burgess is British, his use of "really" simply is different from the use of the adverb in American English. Nonetheless, he does use the adverb more often than the British women writers and it comprises more than half of his total adverb usage. He does use the adverb excessively and he does outdo even the women writers.

If we exclude his sample as being totally idiosyncratic (or perhaps an instance of a man writing in the "feminine" style) and if we consider that three other occurrences of the adverb "really" in the men's fiction are attributed to women speakers, then the use of the adverb by the women fiction writers as contrasted to the men fiction writers is just as high as it is in non-fiction. Its relatively high use by the women writers in both fiction and non-fiction would thus seem to be a characteristic of women's writing.

As commented on earlier, the use of "really" most often indicates doubt—both doubt that one will be believed and doubt that what one is

saying is in fact accurate. Its use may even be one of the "speech characteristics of women" that tend to make them less, not more, believable to
jurors,[3] for the somewhat insistent tone of "really" reflects a need to
prove credibility, to overcome doubt. The women insist on being taken
seriously, simply because they are certain that they are not. The men,
secure in their feeling that they are being taken seriously, that they are
believed, do not need to protest their credibility nearly so often.

Summary

Whereas the men's and women's use of -ly adverbs is not very different
quantitatively, there are many differences qualitatively, especially in fiction. The women use more adverbs of emotion than do the men; the
men use more adverbs of pace than do the women. Within their own
writing, the women use almost the same number of the two types of
adverbs, however, whereas the men use many more adverbs of pace. In
an apparent effort to be credible in the face of disbelief, the women use
the adverb "really" a great deal more often than do the men in both
their fiction and non-fiction. Yet, the women's use of adverbs is much
more consistent both quantitatively and qualitatively in their fiction
and non-fiction than is the men's. The men's use varies considerably
between fiction and non-fiction.

Chapter 8

Women's Words and Men's Words

That men and women employ somewhat different vocabularies is generally accepted. Women, after all, are trained to be polite, to be "nice," to be tactful. They are trained *not* to be "vulgar," *not* to swear or use "dirty" words, *not* to be confronting. The result has been a certain amount of what Kramer calls "wishy-washy Mommy talk,"[1] which is not surprisingly regarded as "weaker" speech than men's. If men's speech is therefore "stronger"–"virile," "aggressive," "macho," "tough," etc.–, for this men receive approbation. Their speech is "stronger" because they are "stronger," which is purportedly as it should be. But women's speech does not receive approval because it ostensibly reflects weakness, and those women who cross over into men's speech usages are automatically considered vulgar or tough. Thus they can gain no approbation by that means either. So, once again, women are caught in a double bind; both their own speech and their use of men's speech are denigrated. Men, on the other hand, use women's talk only at the risk of being considered unmasculine, a fate to be avoided energetically.

Much of the perceived or reported difference doubtless resides in the use of certain adjectives and deserves to be examined. Lakoff[2] cites the following adjectives as used by women only: "cute," "charming," "divine." She refers to these as "empty" adjectives,[3] devoid of any meaning, although it is difficult to see how they are more "empty" than such "neutral" adjectives (i.e., appropriate for use by either men or women) as "terrific" and "neat." All indicate general approbation and all are equally vague. Nonetheless, it is generally held that a particular group of "empty" adjectives is used almost exclusively by women. (There are exceptions, however. Men in the women's fashion industry, for example, can describe a dress as "adorable" with impunity.)

To posit independently a list of adjectives considered to be used exclusively by women is a relatively easy task. Two sections of an undergraduate class in linguistics (50 students of both sexes) were simply asked to jot down those adjectives they felt either were typically used by or pertained to women. Those adjectives occurring on at least five of the lists submitted were included in the study, as follows:

cute	precious
dainty	gentle
delicate	fascinating
dear	horrible
beautiful	suave
charming	dreamy
lovely	wicked
nice	exquisite
sweet	lewd
adorable	serene
divine	frightened

afraid

The list includes but considerably expands Lakoff's list, although hers is not purported to be all-inclusive. More interesting, however, is that the list is by no means confined to "empty" adjectives. Its range reflects the polar views of women as exhibited by the women writers in the study of their similes (see Chapter 6). Nonetheless, all students, both men and women, agreed that these adjectives were the ones they thought most typical of feminine usage. The women students also commented that these were the adjectives that men *thought* women used frequently.

When the same group of students was asked to draw up a list of those adjectives typically used by or pertaining to men, however, the process became much more difficult. There was much puzzlement, uncertainty, and head-scratching. The production of a list of "masculine" adjectives took three times as long as did the production of the "feminine" list. It might be noted that Lakoff herself offers "feminine" adjectives and "neutral" adjectives, but no "masculine" adjectives. It seems that neither the students nor Lakoff knew what a masculine adjective might be, although both the students and Lakoff were very certain about their feminine adjectives. It is apparent that the stereotypes for a minority group—in this case, women—are always easier to perceive than those for a majority group. The focus is on those who are "different" from the majority, and consequently the majority is more difficult to describe. Ultimately, however, the "masculine" adjectives included the following:

strong	powerful
brave	sexy
daring	bitchy
virile	bad
muscular	fine
heroic	terrific
rough	tough
crude	fantastic
handsome	classy
sturdy	attractive

gorgeous

It is clear that there are far more adjectives on the masculine list that are also used easily by women than there are those on the feminine list easily used by men. Such is the proscribed nature of this aspect of women's language, and it is reflected in the findings.

Adjectives in Non-Fiction

In non-fiction, the women use 76 feminine adjectives versus the men's usage of only 30. Twenty-two women use at least one of these adjectives from one to ten times in each sample. Only 15 men use any of the feminine adjectives; those 15 use them from one to five times.

But when it comes to masculine adjectives, the disparity is not nearly so great. All 25 men use at least one of them from one to 18 times, for a total frequency of 163 occurrences. All 25 women non-fiction writers also use the masculine adjectives, from one to 14 times, for a total of 142 occurrences. It seems to be true that women are much freer to use the masculine adjectives than the men are to use the feminine adjectives. But both groups use the masculine adjectives far more often than they use the feminine adjectives. The women use almost twice as many masculine adjectives as feminine adjectives; the men use more than five times as many masculine adjectives.

Those men who use the masculine adjectives most frequently do not use many feminine adjectives. Belz, who uses 18 masculine adjectives, uses no feminine adjectives; Salisbury, who uses 15 masculine adjectives, also uses no feminine adjectives; and Peter, who uses 11 masculine adjectives, uses only three feminine adjectives.

The same selectivity does not obtain in the women's non-fiction writing, where the women who use the greatest number of masculine adjectives also use the feminine adjectives relatively often. DeMille, for example, uses 14 masculine adjectives and seven feminine adjectives; Howar uses 12 masculine adjectives and four feminine adjectives.

Thus, because both the adjectival territories are available to the women, their writing in this respect (as well as in other areas previously noted) is more balanced than that of the men.

Adjectives In Fiction

The range of difference in use of the masculine and feminine adjectives is not so great in fiction as in non-fiction. The men's fiction contains 79 feminine adjectives, used by 21 men from one to ten times. The women's fiction contains 103 feminine adjectives, used by all 25 women from two to six times. The men use more than twice as many feminine adjectives in their fiction as in their non-fiction; the women use only about one and a half times more feminine adjectives in their fiction. That the men employ so many more feminine adjectives in their fiction than in their non-fiction is doubtless due to dialogue representing women's speech.

The men and the women use almost precisely the same number of masculine adjectives in fiction: 132 instances for the women, 128 instances for the men. All 25 men use the masculine adjectives from two to nine times; all 25 women use them from two to eleven times. The preference for the masculine adjectives among the male fiction writers is not so strong as it seems to be in their non-fiction. On the other hand, among the women writers in general, their use of the masculine adjectives is almost exactly the same in their fiction as in their non-fiction.

The Stereotyped Feminine Adjectives

As noted with regard to other aspects of style, quantification does not tell the whole story, however, for it is plain that assumptions have been made concerning both lists of adjectives, particularly the "feminine" list, because the adjectives thereon are much more clearly stereotyped than are those on the masculine list. The 23 adjectives considered "feminine" may indeed be used more frequently by women than by men, but there are many items ("lewd," "fascinating," "frightened," etc.) that are not part of the stereotype. Lakoff would doubtless label them as "neutral." Accordingly, those that *are* most often labeled as typically feminine—the first twelve on the list, from "cute" through "divine"—were studied throughout the entire 200,000 words of prose, with some non-stereotyped results.

The word "cute," for example, is used five times in the men's fiction and never in the women's fiction. Charles Simmons uses the adjective three times, twice in dialogue attributed to a female speaker:

> *I think she's kind of cute . . . .*

> *I still think she's cute . . . .*

followed by a male's utterance:

> *Baby, you're hitting that phase where everything is cute.*

Carter Brown uses the word once, in addressing a woman:

> *Don't give me any of your cute repartee . . . .*

These four instances demonstrate the belief that the word is typical of women's speech. Only Wilfred Sheed attributes the adjective to male speech and uses it to mean "shrewd" or "clever":

Christ, that's a cute idea . . . .

It is perhaps not so noteworthy that the men use the word occasionally in the speech of female characters as it is that the women fiction writers do not themselves use it in the speech of *their* female characters. Thus, if the word "cute" is typical of women's speech (which seems doubtful at best), then it does not carry over into the women's writing or in the women's presentation of their own speech.

Despite Lakoff's report, the word "sweet" also cannot be considered a typical "feminine" adjective; in the fiction sample, the men and the

Table 19. Frequency of Occurrence of Twelve "Feminine" Adjectives: Fiction and Non-Fiction

Adjective	Fiction		Non-Fiction		Total (Fiction and Non-Fiction)	
	Men	Women	Men	Women	Men	Women
cute	5	0	1	2	6	2
adorable	0	0	0	0	0	0
dainty	0	0	0	0	0	0
delicate	1	0	0	0	1	0
dear	2	3	0	1	2	4
beautiful	11	13	4	11	15	24
charming	4	2	0	3	4	5
lovely	2	6	2	9	4	15
sweet	4	4	0	1	4	5
nice	11	16	3	8	14	24
precious	0	0	0	0	0	0
divine	0	0	0	0	0	0
Total	40	44	10	35	50	79

women both use it four times. Parenthetically, the appellations "sweet-ie" and "sweetheart" are used *only* by the men. "Adorable" is simply not used by either group, nor is "divine." A summary of the frequency of occurrence of the twelve adjectives most often attributed to women's language is found in Table 19.

It should be noted that all instances of "dear" used as an appellation, as in "my dear," are eliminated as being appropriate for use by either sex. Also eliminated are all instances of "sweet" and "precious" when used literally. That is, a "sweet" taste is not counted, but a "sweet" appearance or action is. A "precious" stone is only a very valuable stone and is not counted. There are no occurrences of a "precious" person or object where the adjective means "little"/"attractive"/"lovable."

That the differences are very few in fiction is apparent, but in both fiction and non-fiction, three adjectives are used relatively frequently by both the men and the women, although with some greater frequency in the women's writing. They are "beautiful," "lovely," and "nice."

"Beautiful" and "nice," although used somewhat more often by the women fiction writers than by the men fiction writers, are used *far* more often by the women non-fiction writers than by the men non-fiction writers, almost three times as often in each case. The two adjectives are basically terms of approbation and appear to be equally available to both the men and the women, but the proportionately lower frequency of their use by the men non-fiction writers would indicate that the men tend to regard the words as "feminine." "Beautiful" is employed with almost the same frequency by the women fiction and non-fiction writers, whereas the men non-fiction writers use it sparingly—and once in speech attributed to a woman (Lash).

"Nice" is never used by either group in fiction and non-fiction as meaning "precise"; it invariably is a generalized term of approval. One could say, however, that the two adjectives, on a scale of "typically masculine" to "neutral" to "typically feminine," fall somewhere be-tween "neutral" and "typically feminine."

The adjective "lovely" is another matter; it is consistently used with far greater frequency by the women. Overall, in fiction and non-fiction, the women use almost four times as often as do the men. It can justifi-ably be called a "feminine" adjective, but it is the only one on Lakoff's list of which this can be claimed. Thus, if the saccharine adjectives "adorable," "divine," "cute," etc., do occur in women's speech, their usage is not carried over in the women's writing. The women opt instead for the safer and less infantile (but perhaps equally non-specific) adjective "lovely," as exemplified below:

Gordon:

> . . . *the weather's so lovely . . . .*

> . . . *the house looked lovely . . . .*

Lindbergh:

> . . . *a lovely present for me . . . .*

> *It was lovely to be flying myself . . . .*

Holmes:

> *What a lovely thing!*

> . . . *the lovely yellow . . . .*

> . . . *turn out to be shining and good and lovely . . . .*

Newman:

> . . . *isn't she lovely?*

> . . . *it's such a lovely evening . . . .*

> . . . *and the lovely knowledge . . . .*

It is probable, however, that the co-occurrence of "lovely" with other "feminine" adjectives on the list of twelve tends to lend credence to their feminine quality, for only the women use "lovely" at least twice in conjunction with other adjectives on the list. There may be, in other words, a synergistic effect; one or two "lovely"s alone may not seem particularly "feminine," but when the adjective is used in conjunction with others of more questionable "femininity," they are *all* perceived as feminine adjectives.

Nonetheless, only three of the 50 women writers exhibit the pattern of co-occurrence, i.e., two or more "lovely"s plus other random adjectives on the list of twelve. The three women in question and their use of the "feminine" adjectives follow:

Lindbergh: 5 occurrences from the list of twelve
          1 "nice"
          2 "beautiful"
          2 "lovely"

Holmes: 6 occurrences from the list of twelve
          1 "dear"
          1 "beautiful"
          3 "lovely"
          1 "nice"

Gordon: 6 occurrences from the list of twelve
          2 "nice"
          2 "charming"
          2 "lovely"

All three are authors of non-fiction, where the incidence of feminine adjectives is much lower than in fiction. But the nature of their books explains the relatively high use of the feminine adjectives. As remarked previously, Lindbergh's and Gordon's works are autobiographical, although Lindbergh's takes the form of a diary plus some letters. Holmes's book is unclassifiable; it consists of her prayers and pleas to God.

The three are informal and conversational in tone. In their first person narratives, they all indicate an intense effort to be "happy," to see the world pleasantly, despite any feeling to the contrary. (Lindbergh occasionally permits herself to express dismay and hurt. See Chapter 6.) In Holmes's book particularly, there is a good deal of unconscious hostility and anger that she is determined not to recognize. She must "love" her unexpected guests; she must be "happy" scrubbing the kitchen floor; she must be "thankful" for her "dear foolish husband."

These women do not seem to be in touch with their true feelings. They are cheerful and thankful and approving at all costs, and one can only speculate as to what the costs may be. They fulfill only what they imagine their role as women must be, not what it may actually be. They fulfill, as a matter of fact, the images of women that the male writers reveal in their similes concerning women (again see Chapter 6).

In terms of the adjectives used, however, only three of the women are so stoically chirpy; the other 47 women writers do not exhibit such willful romanticism. And, insofar as adjectives are concerned, none of the men does.

Pronouns

As discussed earlier in the chapter, in fiction there is some, but not much, difference in the use by the men and the women of the so-called masculine and feminine adjectives. It is therefore of interest to discover that there is, in fiction, a considerable difference in the use of masculine and feminine pronouns. An investigation of the incidence of "he"/ "his"/"him" and "she"/"hers"/"her" reveals that the women fiction writers employ 1221 feminine pronouns versus only 650 used by the men. This in itself is not surprising. One would expect that women talk more about women than men talk about women in their fiction. But the men fiction writers use the masculine pronouns 1741 times, whereas the women use them 1307 times—a much less marked difference than exists in the use of the feminine pronouns. The women talk about men more often than they talk about women: 1307 masculine pronouns versus 1221 feminine pronouns in their fiction sample. Men, on the other hand, talk about men almost three times as often as they talk about women: 1741 masculine pronouns versus 650 feminine pronouns. On the basis of these pronouns, the women's fiction is far more concerned with men than the men's fiction is with women. The finding is actually a matter of subject matter, where the women once again are the more even-handed. The women's "world" encompasses both sexes; the men's "world" is predominantly masculine. It cannot be said, therefore, that the women's fictional subject matter is narrowly concerned with women, but it can be said that the men's fictional subject is narrowly concerned with men.

And yet the occurrence of the twelve "feminine" adjectives used by the male fiction writers is almost the equal in frequency to that of the women writers. The predominantly masculine subject matter of the men is thus not reflected in their use of adjectives. This apparent contradiction is not a real one, for the men employ the feminine adjectives in their representation of speech *by* women and the women do not (*vide* use of the word "cute").

Verbs

In descriptions of masculine and feminine English language, there are no "masculine" verbs as opposed to "feminine" verbs. But if men are actually more rational and reasonable than women and if women are actually more intuitive and perceptive than men, their verbs expressing thought and intuition may be different. If, for example, women "sense" things that men do not, it is possible that they use that specific verb more often than do the men. Similarly, men might be expected to use the verb "reason" more often than women. In an effort to discern whether these rather pervasive notions have any basis in fact, certain verbs were selected as indicating a reasoning faculty—the "masculine" verbs—and others were chosen that might indicate an intuitive faculty—the "feminine" verbs. The two lists follow:

"Feminine" Verbs	*"Masculine" Verbs*
seem	reason
sense	rationalize
feel	determine
perceive	comprehend
see	pursue
think	prove
guess	work out
imagine	solve
believe	decide
understand	
love	
ponder	
fear	
scare	

That these lists are arbitrary is acknowledged; that they are not really polar is also acknowledged. Some of the verbs may or may not indicate intuition or reasoning. For example, the verb "think" on the "feminine" list may indicate a reasoning process *or* it may indicate conjecture and/or belief. The verb "pursue" on the "masculine" list may or may not indicate intellectual pursuit; it may indicate actual physical pursuit. Furthermore, the "feminine" verbs are generally more common than the "masculine" verbs, which tend to be more Latinate and more formal. Both groups are equally available to men and women, however. That is, there is no stereotype connected with either list. Despite these qualifications, however, differences do exist in their usage by the men and women in the study.

In fiction, all of the men and all of the women use the "feminine" verbs. They occur 310 times in the men's fiction, ranging from three to 23 occurrences per author. They occur 394 times in the women's fiction, with a range of three to 27 occurrences per sample.

As for the "masculine" verbs, they occur, as expected, with far less frequency in the fiction of both groups; the list is shorter and more restrictive. But 20 of the male fiction authors use them a total of 50 times, ranging from one occurrence to six occurrences in the 20 samples. Only 14 women use them for a total of 32 times, with a frequency ranging from one to five occurrences. Thus, in fiction, the women use the "feminine" verbs more often and the "masculine" verbs less often than do the male fiction writers.

In non-fiction, the difference lies chiefly in the "feminine" verbs. All 25 men use them for a total of 259 times, with a range of three to 24 occurrences per author. But all 25 women use the "feminine" verbs 362 times in their non-fiction, with a range of six to 34 occurrences per sample. There is only a slight difference in the "masculine" verbs. Twenty-four male non-fiction writers employ them for a total of 64 instances, ranging from one occurrence to five; 21 women use them a total of 60 times, with a range of one to eight occurrences. These findings are summarized in Table 20.

In both fiction and non-fiction, therefore, the men use more "masculine" verbs than do the women, and in both fiction and non-fiction, the women use more "feminine" verbs than do the men.

Table 20. Frequency of Occurrence of "Masculine" and "Feminine" Verbs: Fiction and Non-Fiction

| | Masculine Verbs | | Feminine Verbs | |
	Occurrences	Authors	Occurrences	Authors
Fiction				
Men	50	20	310	25
Women	32	14	394	25
Non-Fiction				
Men	64	24	259	25
Women	60	21	362	25
Both Categories				
Men	114	44	569	50
Women	92	35	756	50

Thus, despite the arguable nature of the two lists of verbs, there is evidence that the women do "sense" or "perceive" persons/objects/events/meanings more often than do the men, and that they "reason" only slightly less often than the men.

Summary

"Feminine" adjectives are used more often by the women than the men in both fiction and non-fiction, but many of the twelve adjectives considered most stereotypically "feminine" are either not used by either sex or are *not* used more often by the women. Both groups use the "masculine" adjectives more often than "feminine" adjectives. The use of the so-called masculine adjectives does not carry the same pejorative connotations as the use of the so-called feminine adjectives, particularly by men. One specific "feminine" adjective used far more often by the women than by the men is "lovely," which occurs preponderantly in the non-fiction of the women and occasionally in conjunction with the rather less clearly stereotyped "feminine" adjectives, such as "beautiful" and "nice." The co-occurring use of what might be called "pleasant" adjectives ("nice," "dear," "beautiful," "lovely," etc.) probably indicates a need on the part of three of the women writers of non-fiction to suppress their negative impressions of life. In fiction, where the adjective difference between the two groups is less marked, the women's writing as indicated by pronoun usage is nonetheless concerned with both men and women, whereas the men's fiction is concerned predominantly with male figures. And in the verbs suggesting "intuition" and "reasoning," the women consistently employ more of the former but only slightly fewer of the latter in fiction and non-fiction. Thus there are indications that the women intuit considerably more often than the men but do not reason proportionately less often.

Chapter 9

The Feminine Style

Two major questions concerning writing style have been investigated in this study. The findings indicate that women do write differently from men, insofar as the aspects of style dealt with in the study are concerned. Thus it may be cogently claimed that there is indeed a feminine style as opposed to a masculine style.

How women write differently from men is also evidenced by the computer-based findings, and these findings generally lend no credence whatsoever to the popular stereotypes of the feminine style.

First, there is a difference in sentence lengths between the male and female writers, and, contrary to much critical belief, it is the women writers who are comparatively terse and the men who are comparatively long-winded and wordy. Although the average sentence lengths for each group in each category of prose (fiction and non-fiction) are not markedly divergent, close examination reveals that the women consistently write more very short sentences (one to five words) and fewer extremely long sentences (over 70 words) in both fiction and non-fiction. In non-fiction, the women also write many more sentences of from six to 20 words than do the men; in fiction, only their sentences of from 40 to 60 words are significantly more numerous than the men's.

That there is considerable variation of sentence length among the writers in each group is evident. In non-fiction, the average sentence lengths of the individual male writers ranges from 15 to 33 words; in fiction, their sentence lengths range from 13 to 30 words. The average sentence lengths of the individual women writers also range widely, from 12 to 31 words in non-fiction and from 13 to 23 words in fiction. The overall difference of average sentence lengths for each group of writers in both fiction and non-fiction, however, is 17.5 words for the men and only 14.5 words for the women. The women's sentences do not, therefore, vary so much in length as do the men's. As for this particular aspect of style, it can be said that the women's writing is more conservative, less "extreme," and less verbose than the men's.

The women writers also offer a more generalized pattern of complexity in their sentences than do the male authors. In non-fiction, where sentence complexity is pertinent to style, their individual modes of complexity are varied. By contrast, many of the male non-fiction writers favor one particular pattern of complexity. The women writers as a group share patterns of complexity rather than, as individual writers, seize upon one repeated pattern. This trend of diversification in complexity supports the rather "middle-of-the-road" style indicated by the women's sentence lengths.

Second, there is a difference between the men and women writers in both tone (as exemplified by certain types of punctuation) and logical processes of argument. Women's writing has been characterized as "shrill" and "hysterical," as well as "illogical." It is none of these things; yet it does differ from the writing of the men. The differences emerge markedly in non-fiction and not in fiction, although it is usually fiction that is the realm of the traditional male literary critic.

If women writers are indeed shrill and hysterical, one might expect to find evidence of their shrillness and hysteria in a frequent use of exclamation points, for such a punctuator usually indicates surprise, shock, or intense, spontaneous emotion. Nonetheless, it is the male writers who employ half again as many exclamation points as do the women, even though only eleven of the 25 male non-fiction authors use such punctuation at all, as compared with 14 of the female non-fiction authors. The occurrence of one or two exclamation points in 2000 words of text (the size of each author's sample) cannot, of course, be considered evidence of either shrillness or hysteria. Twelve of the 14 women writers use the exclamation point only once or twice; five of the male writers use it only once or twice. With only two exceptions, therefore, the women do not indulge in what might be considered excessive exclamation. And the two women who do employ the exclamation point more than twice (five and seven times respectively) still do not use it as often as the exclamation-point-addicted men, for two of the male authors' samples contain eleven and nine exclamation points, and four other authors use the punctuator from three to five times. The writing style of some of the men, therefore, is distinctly more "shrill" and "hysterical" than that of even the "somewhat hysterical" women writers. Generally speaking, the tone of the women writers is more even, controlled, and moderate than that of the men.

One might ask whether this moderation and comparative *lack* of shrillness on the part of the women writers is supported by any other type of punctuation. Is there, in other words, some other punctuator that functions somehow to express the "opposite" of excitability or sudden emotion? Both the parenthesis and the dash to some degree qualify as the "opposite" of the exclamation point, for both indicate non-essential, unemphasized, and incidental material not associated with excitement.

If the women are found to be comparatively *non*-hysterical and *un*-excitable, they might also modestly deem that more of what they say is, in a sense, disposable. Such is indeed the case. Of the 25 women writers of non-fiction, 19 employ 106 parenthetical expressions and 24 use 179 dashes. Of the 25 male non-fiction writers, 19 use only 79 parentheses, and 22 employ 168 dashes.

More of the women employ parentheses to enclose complete sentences than do the men. Thus, more of the women tend to regard more of their words as non-essential. Although the difference in overall frequency of use of the dash by the men and the women is not great, the men use the dash far more frequently to *summarize* than do the women; the women use it far more often to add on another comment (sometimes a rewording) than do the men.

Thus the comparatively non-hysterical, "unflappable" woman writer tends also to be the modest, somewhat self-abnegating writer, and the comparatively hysterical, "flappable" male writer regards more of what he has to say as essential and indispensable.

Furthermore, contrary to much folk wisdom, women are not illogical; they are only differently logical from men. The women, for example, offer reasons and justifications for their arguments 50 percent more often than do the men; they offer exemplification and conclusions 50 percent *less* often than the men. Offering reasons, causes, and extra information to buttress particular arguments is certainly one way to develop a cogent and logical exposition. That the women's logical processes appear to be less conclusive than those of the men is undeniable. The women's comparative caution in reaching definitive conclusions is not unexpected in the light of other aspects of their style, such as the comparative lack of exclamation, the comparatively large amount of parenthetical material, and the disinclination to use the dash as a summarizing device.

Once again, therefore, the style of the women writers appears conservative, somewhat cautious, and moderate as compared with the style of the men writers.

Third, there is a difference in structural balance and rhetorical effectiveness between the two groups of writers. This is revealed by examining the occurrences of parallelism and concomitant rhetorical devices of repetition in the writing of both groups, for parallelism is evidence of control and one type of syntactic order, at times reinforced by certain devices of repetition. Myth has it that women tend to be psychically "unbalanced"–ergo stylistically unbalanced–whereas men are sane, rational, and balanced–ergo, stylistically balanced. (An "unbalanced" male is often perceived as "inspired"; an "unbalanced" female is merely crazy.)

In the writing style of the two groups in this study, there exists no support for such a myth. Across the two categories of prose, fiction and non-fiction, the two groups use approximately the same number of parallel constructions, with the women exhibiting slightly fewer sentences containing at least one parallelism in their non-fiction and slightly more sentences containing at least one parallelism in their fiction.

If two types of parallelism are disregarded, however, i.e., simple, "obligatory" doublets such as "bacon and eggs" and lengthy, imperceptible parallelisms in many compound sentences, the proportions change considerably. In non-fiction, the men exhibit 479 instances of parallelism; in their fiction, there are 321 such occurrences. The women, however, exhibit 531 instances in their non-fiction and 394 in their fiction. Thus the women writers use parallelism 15 percent more often than do the men, and if parallelism is any kind of measure of a balanced style, the style of the women is *more,* not less, balanced than that of the men.

With regard to those rhetorical devices of repetition that may reinforce structural parallelism, such as polysyndeton, asyndeton, alliteration, and antithesis, the women writers consistently employ them more frequently than do the men in both fiction and non-fiction. Such devices are highly effective and persuasive, whether consciously or unconsciously employed. The men use 314 instances of such devices in their non-fiction and 239 in their fiction. The women, on the other hand, use 369 of these devices in their non-fiction and 349 in their fiction. In terms of total occurrences in each group's writing, the women employ such devices almost 30 percent more often than do the men. In terms of rhetorical effectiveness, as well as balance, therefore, the women's writing outranks that of the men. It is also noteworthy that the women's writing in this respect does not vary between fiction and non-fiction, whereas the devices of repetition sharply decrease in the men's fiction.

Among the specific devices of repetition, however, there is further divergence. The women's non-fiction, for example, contains 51 instances of polysyndeton versus 17 instances in the men's non-fiction. The women's non-fiction also contains more instances of asyndeton—88 instances to the men's 58. These two devices deserve special mention, for their effects are markedly different. Both polysyndeton (the occurrence of repeated conjunctions) and asyndeton (the absence of conjunctions) create uncertainty in the mind of the reader as to when a series will end, for both devices break the "normal" pattern of "comma/comma/comma/'and'," where the "and" indicates the end of a series. Both devices also indicate a lack of subordination, for all items are regarded equally in terms of syntax. Nonetheless, polysyndeton produces an effect of undifferentiated "stringing out," of slowness, of sameness. Asyndeton produces an effect of rapidity, of repeated "hammer blows."

The major differences between the two groups with regard to these devices occurs in non-fiction, as noted above. The two devices are equally used in the fiction of each group, although both polysyndeton and asyndeton are used approximately one-third more often by the women than by the men. In non-fiction, however, the markedly increased use of polysyndeton by the women, as compared to its use by the men, doubtless contributes to a rather non-evaluative, childish quality in some of the women's writing, for it is children who are prone to string together events or items with "and"s regardless of relative importance or emphasis. The flat "sameness" of style of the women writers who employ much polysyndeton probably results from a trained, non-judgmental view of life, from a reluctance to arrive at definite conclusions. Its relatively frequent use by the women is not inconsistent with their comparative lack of conclusions in their logical processes.

Nevertheless, the women non-fiction writers, as noted, also employ more asyndeton than do their male counterparts, and the triphammer effect of this device is in sharp contrast to their use of polysyndeton. The effect of asyndeton is *not* one of repetitive sameness. It is, rather, one of terseness.

The writing of the women, both fiction and non-fiction, encompasses both devices with an increase in the use of asyndeton in their non-fiction. The writing of the men, on the other hand, whereas it also encompasses both devices equally in fiction (albeit with less frequency than that contained in the women's fiction) much more sharply diverges with regard to the use of the two devices in non-fiction. The women use asyndeton only a bit more than two-thirds as often as polysyndeton in their non-fiction; the men use asyndeton almost three and a half times as often as polysyndeton in their non-fiction.

In general, then, the women writers employ both of these devices more evenly than do the men. The flatness, the "life goes on and on" quality of polysyndeton is counterbalanced by the abrupt, sharp, terse effect of asyndeton. The men overwhelmingly prefer the terse, hard effect of asyndeton in their non-fiction.

Also, in the use of these two devices, as with the use of parallelism and other devices of repetition, the writing of the women does not vary between fiction and non-fiction as distinctly as does that of the men, for the women employ both devices 139 times in their non-fiction and 158 times in their fiction, whereas the men use the devices only 75 times in their non-fiction versus 118 times in their fiction.

Thus, in these aspects of style, too—the use of parallel structures and rhetorical devices of repetition—the style of the women is most certainly not unbalanced or extreme. It is balanced, moderate, and even-handed.

Fourth, there is considerable difference between the writing of the men and the writing of the women with regard to the use of similes. Quantitatively, the difference is not startling. The women do use half again as many similes as the men in non-fiction, but the overall incidence of the simile in non-fiction is low. (Both groups employ more similes in their fiction than in their non-fiction.) The quality of the similes in the two non-fiction groups tends to be ideational or visual, rather than emotional. There are more instances of cliché similes in the men's non-fiction than in the women's, despite the fact that the women employ the simile more often. In terms of quality of imagination, therefore, the women non-fiction writers can be said to offer a somewhat higher order than is presented by the men.

And once again, the women's non-fiction and fiction differ less markedly than do those of the men, for the women's fiction contains only half again as many similes as does their non-fiction, compared to the men's fiction, which contains twice as many similes as found in their non-fiction.

It is specifically in the fiction of both groups, however, that distinct, qualitative differences in similes emerge. These differences can be seen most strikingly in those similes employed by either group with reference to men and women. The women's similes concerning themselves and men demonstrate vastly different perceptions of themselves and men from those similes used by the men concerning themselves and women.

As expressed in their similes, the women's views of themselves and of men indicate considerable ambivalence and conflict. Those similes applied to women (by the women) range from highly self-denigrative to threateningly aggressive to completely passive. As a group, the women do not see themselves in any *one* way, although all the similes have negative connotations, for even passivity, albeit approved by men as a mode of behavior for women, cannot be considered a true positive quality. If women thus consider themselves "no good" or "castrating" or quiet and non-"aggressive," these are the views that are internalized by the women writers and brought forth in their fiction.

The women's view of men as evinced in their similes are not so wide-ranging but are more polarized and equally negative. Men are seen to be monsters or monkeys, brutes or fools, to-be-feared or to-be-made-fearful. And throughout the 25,000 words of women's fiction, there is only one simile applied to a man that connotes any sort of admiration. By and large, the "no good" woman or the passive woman is likely to consider men monsters or beasts, whereas the "castrating" or "dominating" woman is likely to perceive men as fools. In all, however, the women writers as a group vary widely in their perceptions of women and are distinctly polarized in their views of men.

These findings are in distinct contrast to the men's similes concerning men and women. The male writers predominantly view women as children, as failed adults. To a lesser degree, they perceive women in romanticized terms—as angels or arpeggios of violins, etc. Both views, of course, are equally unrealistic but certainly contain no evidence of women being perceived as in any way threatening or dangerous. The woman-as-child simile used most often by the men implies that women are helpless, innocent, immature creatures who need the strong, protective aegis of males to survive. There is an overwhelmingly paternalistic perception of themselves revealed in the men's similes for women.

As for the men's similes concerning men, they are as consistent as their similes for women. With one exception, the men view themselves as harmless animals and aging (i.e., impotent) men. Again, there is nothing whatsoever threatening in their perceptions of themselves. Thus the men present women as children and themselves as friendly, asexual beings. Their similes for both men and women are consistent and simple. Their similes for both men and women carry definite implications of complacent belief in their own superiority.

That both the women's and men's similes are derived from internalized views held by a dominant segment of society—male dominance—cannot be seriously questioned. Nowhere, for example, does a woman writer portray a male as a child. But the women's perceptions, confused and conflicted though they may be, are closer to reality than those of men, who are persistently single-minded and simplistic. People and people's perceptions of people in "real life" are often conflicted and complicated. If the women's views of themselves and men are largely negative, they are not only negative in different ways but they are negative because women are a minority group. If the men's similes are largely "positive," the quotation marks are necessary, for such perceptions are falsely positive, flying in the face of fact, and they are "positive" because men are a majority group. Certainly in this aspect of their respective styles, the women's similes are in closer touch with reality than those of the men. The women's uncomfortable views about people reflect life more honestly than do the comfortable views of the men.

Fifth, there is considerable difference between the two groups of writers insofar as certain adverbs are concerned. The difference does not support the common belief that women are "gushier" than men because women employ the hyperbolic adverb (e.g., "utterly divine," "simply dreadful," etc.) far more often than do men. In fact, the two groups use almost exactly the same number of -*ly* adverbs in their prose, with the women's writing containing a few more of such adverbs in their fiction and somewhat fewer in their non-fiction.

There is, however, some difference in the modification patterns of the -*ly* adverbs (that is, *what* such adverbs modify) in the writing of the two groups, but only in the area of fiction and only in adjectival modification, that type of modification most often implied in "gushy" writing. The non-fiction writers of both groups employ adverbs to modify adjectives in almost equal amounts, but in fiction, the men's adverb-modifying-an-adjective pattern drops sharply from that of their non-fiction, whereas the women's adverb-adjective pattern remains almost the same in their fiction as in their non-fiction. Twenty-one percent of the men's non-fiction adverbs modify adjectives, but only 15 percent of their fiction adverbs modify adjectives. The women, on the other hand, use adverbs to modify adjectives in 23 percent of their adverb occurrence in their non-fiction and 21 percent in their fiction. Any claim of women's hyperbolic style with regard to adverb usage thus resides in the comparatively lower number of adverbs used to modify adjectives in the men's fiction. This is a tenuous claim indeed, however, given the fact that the male non-fiction writers employ the adverb-adjective pattern with precisely the same frequency as that of the female fiction writers.

And once more, as with other aspects of style previously discussed (parallelism, rhetorical devices, and similes), the women's fiction and non-fiction styles do not vary so sharply as those of the men.

Certain hyperbolic adverbs attributed to the stereotype of women's style are either in fact used more often by the men than by the women or are used very infrequently by either group. For example, the men use "simply" more often than the women; "utterly" is used infrequently and with equal low frequency by both groups; and "awfully" is used only by the men, but only twice in their entire sample. So much for the stereotyped notions about hyperbolic women.

There are, however, certain adverbs that are used exclusively by the men and others that are used exclusively by the women. As evidenced by 200,000 words of prose, the adverbs "casually," "stiffly," and "thickly" can thus be termed masculine adverbs because only the men use them. The adverbs "bravely," "desperately," "cheerfully," "painfully," "positively," "self-consciously," "unexpectedly," "unwittingly," and "wildly" may by the same token be termed feminine adverbs, because only the women use them. Even though the list of feminine adverbs is longer than that of the masculine adverbs, the comparatively longer list does not, as previously noted, indicate that the women use significantly more adverbs in general. The women's list only indicates that more adverbs seem to be considered in their province of language and fewer specific adverbs seem to be considered solely in the province of masculine language. The disparity in the length of the two lists, therefore, is not particularly meaningful.

It is, however, in the quality of the two lists that a very marked difference is evident. The men's adverbs are emotionally detached; the women's are most definitely not detached. The women's adverbs are filled with emotion and effort, and the emotions indicated range from very negative expressions to very positive ones. There is nothing, in other words, "casual" about the women's adverbs, and there is everything "casual" about the men's adverbs.

Investigation of all the adverbs of emotion in the two groups of writers supports the qualities found in the two mutually exclusive lists cited above. In non-fiction, the men and the women use the same number of adverbs of emotion (34 in each group), but in fiction, the women use more than twice as many as the men, with 49 instances as compared to 23 in the men's fiction. The women's use of the adverbs of emotion increases in their fiction in almost precisely the same proportion as the men's use of such adverbs decreases in their fiction. By comparison to the men's fiction style, the women's is therefore more emotional.

If such is the case, however, one might well ask whether the men's style is more "active" than that of the women. Implicit in the question is the notion that a comparative lack of emotion might co-occur with a comparative increase in concern with physical action. Such does indeed seem to be the case, for investigation of the adverbs of pace (e.g., "quickly," "slowly," etc.) reveals that the men use such adverbs far more often than the women (86 instances as compared to the women's 50), with the difference again occurring in the fiction of the two groups and no difference in their non-fiction. There is then a distinct concern with the quality of action in the men's fiction as opposed to the more evident quality of emotion in the women's fiction.

Nonetheless, it cannot be claimed that the women's fiction style is "hyperemotional," for the women, in their repeatedly evenhanded way, use almost exactly the same number of adverbs of emotion and adverbs of pace in their fiction. It is, rather, that the men's fiction is markedly "hypoemotional," for the men employ almost four times more adverbs of pace than adverbs of emotion.

Not only is the women's use of the two types of adverbs balanced in their fiction, their use of the two types does not vary from fiction to non-fiction so greatly as does the men's. The women's fiction contains 15 more instances of adverbs of emotion than does their non-fiction; their fiction contains 15 more adverbs of pace than contained in their non-fiction. The men's fiction contains 11 *fewer* adverbs of emotion than their non-fiction and 54 *more* adverbs of pace than in their non-fiction. It is clear that in this aspect of style as well as others already discussed, the women's non-fiction and fiction styles vary far less than do those of the men.

One further difference between the two groups in their use of adverbs centers upon one particular adverb – "really." The writing of both groups contains "really"; it is not exclusive to either group. But the women writers use it almost three times as often as the men in non-fiction writing and markedly more often in fiction. The use of the word generally connotes doubt on the part of the speaker/writer that he or she will be believed. (In this study, it is rarely used literally, as in, "It looked like a bird, but it was really a plane.") The writer who does not expect to be believed is somehow compelled to offer an emphatic statement that something is not merely "true"; it is "*really* true." That the women writers are afflicted by doubts as to their credibility is evident in their comparatively high use of "really." This is not an irrational doubt, however, for the veracity and accuracy of women's statements are far more often called into question than those of men's statements. Men, after all, are *the* authority. The frequent use of the word, however, tends to convey an over-protestation that raises rather than lowers the threshhold of credibility. In other words, a plethora of "really"s may not only *not* reassure an audience or reader that what is being said is true; it may actually create doubts as to veracity, for why else, presumably, would the word be necessary? For this reason, therefore, the high frequency of the adverb in the women's writing as compared to that of the men perhaps does indicate a doubt on the part of the woman writer not only that she may not be believed but also that what she is averring to be true may in fact not be true.

There is, then, a double-bind to which the frequent user of the adverb is subjected. First, she may use the adverb because she perceives a non-believing world. Second, she may use the adverb because she perceives self-doubts. It is probably fair to say that, as a group, the women entertain both kinds of doubts more often than do the men. It is probably more accurate to say that the women *reveal* both kinds of doubts more often than do the men.

In either case, there is a lack of certainty connoted by the word, and its more frequent use by the women supports their lack of a fixed perception of themselves and of men evidenced in their similes. As with the similes, however, such perception is more realistic than that of the men and is certainly to be expected in any minority group.

The *final* aspects of style examined in the study have to do with adjectives, pronouns, and verbs as used by the men and the women. And again, the findings indicate differences, but, also again, the differences do not support stereotyped ideas despite the fact that the two sexes are trained to use different vocabularies.

As we all know, women are taught not to use "vulgar" language but instead to use "polite" words. Only men can "talk tough." It is a common notion, therefore, that women are the typical users of such adjectives as "cute," "adorable," "charming," "divine," etc., and that men do *not* use such adjectives. The fact that it is relatively easy to discover a list of adjectives perceived as typically "feminine" and relatively difficult to arrive at a list of those considered typically "masculine" only underscores the singling out of "minority" language for comment and notice.

Two lists of adjectives considered "feminine" and "masculine" respectively, however, do offer some insights into the actual usage of such adjectives by the two groups of writers. In non-fiction, both groups use the so-called masculine adjectives more frequently than they use the so-called feminine adjectives, although the men use the masculine adjectives five times as often as they use the feminine adjectives. The women, by comparison, use almost twice as many masculine adjectives as feminine adjectives. Conversely, therefore, the women non-fiction writers do use the feminine adjectives more often than do the men. But once again, the women do not display the same selectivity as do the men, two of whom use *no* feminine adjectives. The women tend to use both types.

In fiction, there is less difference between the two groups. The men, doubtless because of the occurrence of representation of female speech, use more feminine adjectives than they do in their non-fiction. Both the men and the women use almost exactly the same number of masculine adjectives. Furthermore, the number of masculine adjectives used by the women in both fiction and non-fiction is almost exactly the same. Their use of the feminine adjectives increases by 27 instances in their fiction over their non-fiction, whereas the men's use of the feminine adjectives in fiction increases by 49 instances over their non-fiction.

Because both the focus and folk-lore are centered on the feminine adjectives, a list of twelve such adjectives considered most "typical" of women's speech and writing was drawn up. The women do use them more often than do the men (79 occurrences in the women's writing versus 50 in the men's), but the chief divergence lies in non-fiction, rather than in fiction. In non-fiction, the women use these adjectives three times as often as do the men. The previously mentioned representation of feminine speech in the men's fiction doubtless accounts for the very small difference in this category. And neither the women nor the men use *all* twelve of these "typically" feminine adjectives in either category of prose.

Thus it is noteworthy that the stereotypically feminine "cute" is used five times in the men's fiction and never in the women's fiction. The word is doubtless considered by the male writer to be "feminine," but it is not used by the women themselves at all. "Adorable" and "divine" are not used by either group; the two words are, then, certainly not "feminine" adjectives. "Charming" is used equally by both groups; it also is not typically "feminine." Two other adjectives on the list of twelve—"beautiful" and "nice"—might better be considered neutral, for, although they are used 24 times each by the women, they are also used relatively frequently by the men, with 15 and 14 occurrences respectively. Only one adjective on the list of twelve is used by the women much more frequently than by the men. This is the adjective "lovely," found in the women's writing 15 times and in the men's only four times. It can thus justifiably be termed a "feminine" adjective. It indicates generalized approbation; it is non-specific, as are "beautiful" and "nice." But it is not childish, as is "cute," which the men seem to *think* women use.

With regard to the use of the masculine pronouns "he"/"his"/"him" and the feminine pronouns "she"/"hers"/"her," as contained in the fiction sample, it is a slightly less than stunning finding that, on the basis of these pronouns, the male writers talk three times more often about men than about women and that the women talk about men approximately ten percent more often than about women. In other words, the fictional subject matter of both groups concerns men more often than women. But once again, the women's subject matter is more balanced, for the women writers do encompass both sexes in their "world" almost equally, as contrasted to the overwhelmingly masculine "world" of the male fiction writers. The use of these pronouns is, of course, not strictly a matter of style. But the findings do refute the notion that women's fiction is predominantly concerned with women. Rather, they support a view that men's fiction is narrowly concerned with men.

As far as the use of verbs is concerned, there are no stereotyped ideas of "femininity" or "masculinity." Nonetheless, it *is* a prevailing notion that men are the rational and women are the intuitive writers. If such is the case, the women might be expected to "sense" things more often than the men and the men might be expected to "reason" more often than the women.

On the basis of two quite arbitrary, not distinctly polar, lists, there is some support for the "rational" man and the "intuitive" woman. In the entire sample of 200,000 words, the men use 114 "masculine" verbs versus the women's use of 92; the men use 569 "feminine" verbs versus the women's use of 756. Thus it would seem that the women use reason only somewhat less often than the men, but they intuit considerably more often than the men.

From a consideration of all the aspects of style covered in the study, a profile of women's writing style emerges. Individual writers in each group may vary from the predominant style of each group, but the profile of the women's writing is quite different from that of the men—and it is also quite different from many hackneyed sexist impressions of women's style. In fact, the way women write is quite the opposite of the way they are frequently thought to write. Far from presenting a "shrill" tone, a rambling, "irrational," "hysterical," "hyperemotional," or disorganized style, they show themselves to be moderate in tone as compared to the men, well-balanced, rational, organized, and "unextreme" in almost every aspect of their writing style. As compared to their male counterparts, their style is rhetorically more effective at the same time that it is more conservative in other aspects of expression. It is, in general, a middle-of-the-road style, not given to extremes of length or brevity, not given to extremes of emotion or action, not given to extemes of "feminine" concerns to the exclusion of "masculine" concerns.

Furthermore, the way women write reflects a more varied perception of the world than that held by men and their style embraces more varied syntactic structures than that of the men. Their style is, in other words, less fixated and narrow than that of the men in terms of perception, fictional subject matter, and sentence structure.

The fiction style of the women is consistently more consonant with their non-fiction style than is that of the men. It is the writing of the men that displays sharp divergences between fiction and non-fiction, between length and brevity, between emotion and action. It is the men's style that display narrowness of fictional concerns, simplistic perceptions, and "hypoemotionality."

But it is men's writing that is considered the "standard" and the majority carries more weight than the minority. If, therefore, the "standard" style is discovered to be lacking in emotional expression, the "non-standard" or minority style is thus deviant and automatically judged excessively emotional. If, in other words, the masculine style is taken as the standard, and it unfortunately is so taken, then apprehension of the minority style is seriously distorted, so that what is not "*hypo*emotional" is regarded automatically as "hyperemotional," despite evidence to the contrary. The women's style is in fact more conservative and less extreme than that of the men. The excesses of which women writers are so often accused are derived only from judgments founded on a comparison with the masculine "standard."

One might ask *why* is the way women write more moderate, consistent, and even-handed than the way men write?

The chief reason is doubtless that women are a minority group, more likely to conform than to dare. From infancy, women are trained to conform in all areas of behavior; men are often admired for being rebellious. For women, the act of writing is in itself probably something of a rebellion in that writing is active and self-expressive, whereas they have been told that they should be passive and keep their opinions to themselves. In the "rebellion" of their writing, however, the women remember the rules of behavior: Don't scream or shout; don't natter on and on; don't be arrogant; don't be repetitious; don't be curt; don't be self-pitying; don't jump to conclusions; don't be unreasonable; etc. Under the circumstances, it is to be expected that they seem at times unsure that anyone will believe them, reluctant to arrive at conclusions, and a bit overdetermined to present a cheerful face.

The women's style is also more perceptive than that of the men, and the reason for that is that women, as a minority group, probably learn to rely on their perceptions and feelings because they are denied access to a world of action, "big" decisions, and authority. Thus they strive, often unsuccessfully, to see the world happily, but they also see the world as confusing, conflicting, and hostile. Their range of emotions is far wider than that presented by the men, for it encompasses love *and* anger. They are not nearly so exclusively preoccupied with action as are the men. They reason as often as the men, but they do intuit more often. They are, in a word, more sensitive but not less rational than the men. They perceive themselves and men in a variety of ways, thus acknowledging that there is indeed much variety. The men, by contrast, deny the truth, either consciously or unconsciously, in their simplistic views of themselves and women, perhaps because their "world" of action emphasizes events and decisions rather than perceptive observations of people.

Epilogue

In many ways, the nature of much criticism of the feminine style is revealed to be unfair and distorted, because most often men have done the judging and based their judgments on the standard of masculine style.

Sexist criticism of the feminine style has a long history. Thus it was in the beginning. Thus it has been. Is it still thus?

The last question posed can perhaps be answered with guarded optimism. Thus it still perhaps is, but there are indications that male literary critics have become aware that previously expressed opinions about the feminine style are at least open to question. *Item:* In one issue of the *New York Times Book Review* (August 8, 1976), eight of the ten books written by women are reviewed by women, although the books are all subsumed under the heading: "Women." *Item:* John Updike's review of novels by Gayl Jones and Christina Stead (*The New Yorker,* August 9, 1976) concludes as follows: "If there is such a thing as a 'woman's novel,' it finds itself bound, at least in the honest hands of Mss. Stead and Jones, to the figurative description not of an action but of a quality—the quality of femininity, static and wary, hugging to itself the bleak dignity of solitude." *Item:* Clive Barnes, in his introductory remarks concerning a play by Marguerite Duras (*New York Times,* September 28, 1976), observes: "There is something curiously insulting about the phrase 'woman novelist'—perhaps because no one has ever suggested that there could be a 'man novelist'."

That these items reveal both pluses and minuses is evident. Whereas indications of the increased number of women reviewing women's books are to be applauded, there is considerable sexism in assigning the books to a special division entitled "Women." Likewise, Updike is to be commended for his awareness that there is a question concerning "a woman's novel," but his remarks about the "quality of femininity" reveal lack of judgment and insight. And, although Barnes can be given a nod of approval for the exception taken to the term "woman novelist," he curiously finds such exception to be "curious."

As far as critical opinion regarding women's books is concerned, therefore, there are indications that the male critic's consciousness has been somewhat raised. And the question of the *persistence* of dominatingly sexist criticism of women's style can be answered, cautiously and inelegantly, "Thus perhaps it still is, but it's not so bad as it was in the beginning."

Notes

Chapter 1

[1] Fraya Katz-Stoker, "Feminism vs. Formalism," in *Images of Women in Fiction,* ed. Susan Koppelman Cornillon (Bowling Green, Ohio: Popular Press, 1972), p. 324.

[2] Cited by Elaine Showalter, "Women Writers and the Double Standard," in *Women in Sexist Society,* eds. Vivian Gornick and Barbara K. Moran (New York: Signet-New American Library, 1971), pp. 464-465.

[3] Carol Ohmann, "Emily Brontë in the Hands of Male Critics," *College English* 32 (May 1971), p. 906.

[4] Grant C. Knight, *James Lane Allen and the Genteel Tradition* (Chapel Hill: University of North Carolina Press, 1935), pp. 114-115.

[5] Cited by Carolyn Heilbrun, *Toward a Recognition of Androgyny* (New York: Harper and Row, 1973), p. xvii.

[6] Walter Pater, *Plato and Platonism* (New York: Macmillan Co., 1899), p. 253.

[7] Otto Jespersen, *Language* (London: George Allen and Unwin, Ltd., 1922, rpt. 1928), p. 247.

[8] Cited by Wendy Martin, "The Image of Woman in American Fiction," in *Women in Sexist Society,* p. 335.

[9] Jacques Barzun and Wendell Hertig Taylor, *A Catalogue of Crime* (New York: Harper and Row, 1971), p. 12.

[10] *Ibid.,* p. 13.

[11] Norman Mailer, *Advertisements for Myself* (New York: G. P. Putnam's Sons, 1959), p. 472.

[12] Leslie A. Fiedler, *Love and Death in the American Novel* (New York: Criterion Books, 1960), pp. 54-56.

[13] Quoted by Mary Ellmann, *Thinking About Women* (New York: Harcourt, Brace, Jovanovich, 1968), p. 150.

[14] David Bromwich, Review of Penelope Mortimer's *Long Distance,*

New York Times Book Review, 22 September 1974, p. 3. A careful search through extant English dictionaries fails to reveal the word *femid.* One can only guess that the word *fumid* was intended.

[15] Advertisement quoting *John Barkham Reviews, New York Times,* 27 February 1976.

[16] Auberon Waugh, review in *New York Times Book Review,* 9 May 1976, p. 8.

[17] Anthony Burgess, "The Book Is Not for Reading," *New York Times Book Review,* 4 December 1966, p. 1, 74.

[18] William Gass, Review of Norman Mailer's *Genius and Lust, New York Times Book Review,* 24 October 1976, p. 2.

[19] Jane Aiken Hodge, *Only a Novel* (New York: Fawcett, 1973), p. 245.

[20] Quoted by Elaine Showalter, "Women Writers and the Double Standard," in *Women in Sexist Society,* p. 477.

[21] Quoted by Patricia Beer, in a review of Patricia Mayer Spacks' *The Female Imagination, New York Times Book Review,* 11 May 1975, pp. 42-43.

[22] Quoted by Norma Rosen, "Who's Afraid of Erica Jong?", *New York Times Magazine,* 28 July 1974, p. 8. Rosen, in "American Scholar Forum," also comments on a woman painter who "consciously evolved a style that is as, quote, unfeminine as possible: strong, bold, hard–." *American Scholar* 41 (Autumn 1972), p. 610.

[23] Ellmann, *Thinking About Women,* p. 172.

[24] Review of *On Being Told That Her Second Husband Has Taken His First Lover, New York Times Book Review,* 13 October 1974, p. 31.

[25] Heilbrun, *Toward a Recognition of Androgyny,* p. xiv.

[26] References have been made to all except Kate Millett, *Sexual Politics* (New York: Avon Publishers, 1971).

[27] Carolyn Heilbrun, "Speaking of Susan Sontag," *New York Times Book Review,* 27 August 1967, p. 30. See also Ellmann, *Thinking About Women,* p. 208.

[28] Ellmann, *Thinking About Women,* pp. 207-208.

[29] Josephine Donovan, "Feminist Style Criticism," in *Images of Women in Fiction,* p. 352.

[30] Review excerpt quoted in *New York Times,* 16 July 1976, of Norman MacLean, *A River Runs Through It* (Chicago: University of Chicago Press, 1976).

[31] Karl Kroeber, *Styles in Fictional Structure* (Princeton: Princeton University Press, 1971), p. 182.

[32] *Ibid.,* p. 184.

[33] *E.g.,* Louis T. Milic, "Against the Typology of Styles," in *Essays on the Language of Literature,* eds. Seymour Chatman and Samuel R. Levin (Boston: Houghton Mifflin Company, 1967), pp. 442-450.

[34] Ellmann, *Thinking About Women,* pp. 28-54.

[35] Annette Kolodny, "Some Notes on Defining a 'Feminist Literary Criticism'," *Critical Inquiry* 2 (Autumn 1975), p. 78.

[36] *Ibid., p.* 87.

[37] Robin Lakoff, *Language and Woman's Place* (New York: Harper and Row, 1975).

[38] *Ibid., p.* 4.

[39] Mary Ritchie Key, *Male/Female Language* (Metuchen, N.J.: The Scarecrow Press, 1975).

[40] *Ibid.,* p. 87.

[41] Cheris Kramer, "Actual and Perceived Sex-Linked Differences in Adverb and Adjective Usage," presented at the Annual Meeting of the Linguistic Society of America, San Diego, California, 28-30 December 1973.

[42] Cheris Kramer, "Women's Speech: Separate But Unequal?", *Quarterly Journal of Speech* 20 (February 1974), pp. 14-24.

[43] Cheris Kramer, "Folk-Linguistics: Wishy-Washy Mommy Talk," *Psychology Today* 8 (June 1974), pp. 82-85.

[44] Diana W. Warshay, "Sex Differences in Language Style," in *Toward a Sociology of Women,* ed. Constantina Safilos-Rothschild (Lexington, Mass.: Xerox Publishing Company, 1972), pp. 3-9.

[45] William Nichols, "Skeptics and Believers: The Science-Humanities Debate," *The American Scholar* 45 (Summer 1976), p. 378.

[46] *Ibid.,* pp. 378-379.

[47] *Ibid.,* p. 386.

Chapter 2

[1] Gender of authors was determined by name. Where there existed an uncertainty, the author's publisher was contacted. In the sample, only one author is an avowed homosexual. There may be other, unavowed

homosexuals included in the 100 authors. But whether and how sexual preferences influence style is the subject of a separate study.
[2] Henry Kučera and W. Nelson Francis, *Computational Analysis of Present-Day American English* (Providence: Brown University Press, 1967).
[3] A similar and more rapid programing language is SPITBOL, but because most of the programs had been written using SNOBOL before SPITBOL became available, the time lost in rewriting and "rerunning" the programs was not thought justified by the computer time saved by SPITBOL.
[4] Ben Ross Schneider's involvement with the *London Stage* Information Bank Project uses this approach. His often hilarious account of his direction of and experiences in the project, which included keypunching in Hong Kong, programing in Wisconsin, and editing in London, can be found in his *Travels in Computerland* (Reading, Mass.: Addison Wesley Publishing Co., 1974).

Chapter 3

[1] Ellmann, *Thinking About Women*, pp. 153-174.
[2] All exemplifications are from the random selections (see Appendix) that make up the 200,000-word corpus and are discovered by computer. Specific page references for these are considered only remotely useful. In the interest of eliminating a plethora of footnotes, they are not included.

Chapter 4

[1] Louis T. Milic, *Stylists on Style* (New York: Charles Scribner's Sons, 1969), pp. 21-22.

Chapter 5

[1] Ellmann, *Thinking About Women*, p. 86.
[2] Leo Lowenthal, *Literature and the Image of Man* (Boston: Beacon Press, 1957), p. 17.
[3] See my *Artful Balance: The Parallel Structures of Style* (New York: Teachers College Press, 1975) for a detailed study of parallelism in contemporary prose.

Chapter 7

[1] Otto Jespersen, *Language: Its Nature, Development, and Origin,* p. 250.
[2] Kramer, "Actual and Perceived Sex-Linked Differences in Adverb and Adjective Usage."
[3] "Verdicts Linked to Speech Style," *New York Times,* 14 December 1975, p. 38. Findings reported at American Anthropological Association meeting, San Francisco.

Chapter 8

[1] Kramer, "Folk-Linguistics: Wishy-Washy Mommy Talk."
[2] Lakoff, *Language and Woman's Place,* p. 53.
[3] *Ibid.*

Bibliography

Barzun, Jacques, and Taylor, Wendell Hertig. *A Catalogue of Crime.* New York: Harper and Row, 1971.

Beer, Patricia. Review of Patricia Mayer Spacks' *The Female Imagination. New York Times Book Review,* 11 May 1975, pp. 42-43.

Bromwich, David. Review of Penelope Mortimer's *Long Distance. New York Times Book Review,* 22 September 1974, p. 3.

Burgess, Anthony. "The Book Is Not for Reading." *New York Times Book Review,* 4 December 1966, pp. 1, 74.

Donovan, Josephine. "Feminist Style Criticism." In *Images of Women in Fiction,* edited by Susan Koppelman Cornillon. Bowling Green, Ohio: Popular Press, 1972.

Ellmann, Mary. *Thinking About Women.* New York: Harcourt, Brace, Jovanovich, 1968.

Fiedler, Leslie A. *Love and Death in the American Novel.* New York: Criterion Books, 1960.

Gass, William. Review of Norman Mailer's *Genius and Lust. New York Times Book Review,* 24 October 1976, pp. 1-3.

Gottlieb, Annie. Review of *On Being Told That Her Second Husband Has Taken His First Lover. New York Times Book Review,* 13 October 1974, pp. 31ff.

Heilbrun, Carolyn. "Speaking of Susan Sontag." *New York Times Book Review,* 27 August 1967, p. 30.

——————— . *Toward a Recognition of Androgyny.* New York: Harper and Row, 1973.

Hiatt, Mary P. *Artful Balance: The Parallel Structures of Style.* New York: Teachers College Press, 1975.

Hodge, Jane Aiken. *Only a Novel.* New York: Fawcett, 1973.

Jespersen, Otto. *Language.* London: George Allen and Unwin, Ltd., 1922, rpt. 1928.

John Barkham Reviews. Advertisement in *New York Times,* 27 February 1976.

Katz-Stoker, Fraya. "Feminism vs. Formalism." In *Images of Women in Fiction,* edited by Susan Koppelman Cornillon. Bowling Green, Ohio: Popular Press, 1972.

Key, Mary Ritchie. *Male/Female Language.* Metuchen, N.J.: The Scarecrow Press, 1975.

Knight, Grant C. *James Lane Allen and the Genteel Tradition.* Chapel Hill: University of North Carolina Press, 1935.

Kolodny, Annette. "Some Notes on Defining a 'Feminist Literary Criticism'." *Critical Inquiry* 2 (Autumn 1975): 75-92.

Kramer, Cheris. "Actual and Perceived Sex-Linked Differences in Adverb and Adjective Usage." Presented at the Annual Meeting of the Linguistic Society of America, San Diego, Calif., 28-30 December 1973.

_____ . "Folk-Linguistics: Wishy-Washy Mommy Talk." *Psychology Today* 8 (June 1974): 82-85.

_____ . "Women's Speech: Separate But Unequal?" *Quarterly Journal of Speech* 20 (February 1974): 14-24.

Kroeber, Karl. *Styles in Fictional Structure.* Princeton: Princeton University Press, 1971.

Kučera, Henry, and Francis, W. Nelson. *Computational Analysis of Present-Day American English.* Providence: Brown University Press, 1967.

Lakoff, Robin. *Language and Woman's Place.* New York: Harper and Row, 1975.

Lowenthal, Leo. *Literature and the Image of Man.* Boston: Beacon Press, 1957.

MacLean, Norman. *A River Runs Through It.* Chicago: University of Chicago Press, 1976. Advertisement in *New York Times,* 16 July 1976.

Mailer, Norman. *Advertisements for Myself.* New York: G. P. Putman's Sons, 1959.

Martin, Wendy. "The Image of Woman in American Fiction." In *Woman in Sexist Society,* edited by Vivian Gornick and Barbara K. Moran. New York: Signet-New American Library, 1971.

Milic, Louis T. "Against the Typology of Styles." In *Essays on the Language of Literature,* edited by Seymour Chatman and Samuel R. Levin. Boston: Houghton Mifflin Company, 1967.

—————. *Stylists on Style.* New York: Charles Scribner's Sons, 1969.

Millett, Kate. *Sexual Politics.* New York: Avon Publishers, 1971.

Nichols, William. "Skeptics and Believers: The Science-Humanities Debate." *The American Scholar* 45 (Summer 1976): 377-386.

Ohmann, Carol. "Emily Brontë in the Hands of Male Critics." *College English* 32 (May 1971): 906-913.

Pater, Walter. *Plato and Platonism.* New York: Macmillan Co., 1899.

Rosen, Norma. "American Scholar Forum." *American Scholar* 41 (Autumn 1972): 599-627.

—————. "Who's Afraid of Erica Jong?" *New York Times Magazine,* 28 July 1974, pp. 8ff.

Schneider, Ben Ross. *Travels in Computerland.* Reading, Mass.: Addison Wesley Publishing Co., 1974.

Showalter, Elaine. "Women Writers and the Double Standard." In *Woman in Sexist Society,* edited by Vivian Gornick and Barbara K. Moran. New York: Signet-New American Library, 1971.

Thorne, Barrie, and Henley, Nancy, eds. *Language and Sex: Difference and Dominance.* Rowley, Mass.: Newbury House, 1975.

"Verdicts Linked to Speech Style." *New York Times,* 14 December 1975, p. 38.

Warshay, Diana W. "Sex Differences in Language Style." In *Toward a Sociology of Women,* edited by Constantina Safilos-Rothschild. Lexington, Mass.: Xerox Publishing Company, 1972.

Waugh, Auberon. Review in *New York Times Book Review,* 9 May 1976, pp. 8ff.

APPENDIX

Books Used as Basis of the Study

Aiken, Joan. *The Fortune Hunters.* New York: Pocket Books, 1973. Pp. 33-34, 79-80, 99-100,113-114.

Albrand, Martha. *Wait for the Dawn.* New York: Avon Books, 1973. Pp. 40-42, 78-79, 111-112, 169-170.

Alpert, Hollis. *The Summer Lovers.* New York: Bantam Books, Inc., 1973. Pp. 73-74, 111-112, 149-150, 216-217.

Arnold, Elliott. *Walk with the Devil.* New York: Pyramid Books, 1973. Pp. 66-68, 119-121, 155-156, 196-197.

Belz, Carl. *The Story of Rock.* New York: Harper & Row Publishers, Inc., 1971. Pp. 13-15, 60-62, 136-138, 181-182.

Bing, Rudolf. *5000 Nights at the Opera.* New York: Popular Library, 1972. Pp. 85-86, 159-160, 236-237, 277-278.

Block, Jean Libman. *Telfair's Daughter.* New York: Bantam Books, Inc., 1974. Pp. 19-20, 47-48, 94-95, 152-153.

Boyd, Alice. *Two People.* New York: Dell Publishing Co., Inc., 1973. Pp. 41-43, 64-66, 116-119, 152-154.

Breen, Mike. *Zachary.* New York: Popular Library, 1974. Pp. 69-70, 111-112, 174-175, 212-213.

Brothers, Joyce. *The Brothers System for Liberated Love and Marriage.* New York: Avon Books, 1973. Pp. 53-54, 92-93, 141-142, 217-218.

Brown, Carter. *The Jade-Eyed Jungle.* New York: New American Library, 1963. Pp. 41-42, 52-53, 87-88, 113-115.

Buchanan, Marie. *Anima.* Greenwich, Conn.: Fawcett Publications, Inc., 1973. Pp. 65-68, 88-90, 140-142, 177-179.

Burgess, Anthony. *One Hand Clapping*. New York: Ballantine Books, Inc., 1973. Pp. 30-31, 69-70, 113-114, 136-137.

Carey, Gary. *Brando!* New York: Pocket Books, 1973. Pp. 85-86, 121-122, 155-157, 196-198.

Carlino, Lewis John. *The Mechanic*. New York: New American Library, 1972. Pp. 33-34, 74-76, 96-98, 123-124.

Cartland, Barbara. *Josephine, Empress of France*. New York: Pyramid Books, 1974. Pp. 46-47, 79-81, 112-113, 158-159.

Cartwright, Frederick F. *Disease and History*. New York: New American Library, 1974. Pp. 65-66, 113-114, 152-153, 189-190.

Chesler, Phyllis. *Women and Madness*. New York: Avon Books, 1973. Pp. 79-81, 153-155, 218-219, 263-264.

Clark, Ronald. *Einstein: The Life and Times*. New York: Avon Books, 1972. Pp. 168-169, 249-250, 411-412, 619-620.

Cohen, Susan. *Liberated Marriage*. New York: Lancer Books, Inc., 1971. Pp. 34-36, 82-83, 111-113, 131-132.

DeMille, Agnes. *Speak to Me, Dance with Me*. New York: Popular Library, 1973. Pp. 73-75, 158-160, 239-241, 315-316.

Didion, Joan. *Play It as It Lays*. New York: Farrar, Straus, and Giroux, 1970. Pp. 60-62, 75-78, 140-143, 187-190.

Drexler, Rosalyn. *To Smithereens*. New York: New American Library, 1972. Pp. 58-59, 92-93, 108-109, 159-160.

DuMaurier, Daphne. *The Glass Blowers*. New York: Avon Books, 1971. Pp. 81-82, 124-125, 207-208, 264-265.

Edwards, Frank. *Strange People*. New York: New American Library, 1974. Pp. 56-57, 79-80, 129-130, 160-161.

Ellis, Albert. *The Sensuous Person*. New York: New American Library, 1974. Pp. 45-46, 61-62, 99-100, 124-125.

Fairbairn, Ann. *Five Smooth Stones*. New York: Bantam Books, Inc., 1968. Pp. 148-149, 309-310, 444-445, 668-669.

Farmer, Frances. *Will There Really Be a Morning?* New York: Dell Publishing Co., Inc., 1973. Pp. 93-94, 179-180, 236-237, 296-297.

Fisher, Florence. *The Search for Anna Fisher*. Greenwich, Conn.: Fawcett Publications, Inc., 1973. Pp. 76-77, 97-98, 135-136, 165-166.

FitzGerald, Frances. *Fire in the Lake*. New York: Random House, Inc., 1973, Pp. 93-94, 221-223, 349-350, 448-449.

Friday, Nancy. *My Secret Garden.* New York: Pocket Books, 1974. Pp. 2-4, 21-23, 91-92, 198-199.

Gilbert, Edwin. *Newport.* New York: Bantam Books, Inc., 1972. Pp. 59-60, 115-116, 168-170, 214-215.

Goodavage, Joseph. *The Comet Kohoutek.* New York: Pinnacle Books, Inc., 1973. Pp. 47-49, 69-71, 98-100, 144-146.

Gordon, Ruth. *Myself Among Others.* New York: Dell Publishing Co., Inc., 1970. Pp. 94-95, 125-126, 235-236, 274-275.

Gould, Lois. *Necessary Objects.* New York: Dell Publishing Co., Inc., 1973. Pp. 82-83, 125-127, 198-200, 236-238.

Grau, Shirley Ann. *The Black Prince.* Greenwich, Conn.: Fawcett Publications, Inc., 1973. Pp. 76-77, 112-113, 134-135, 181-182.

Greene, Graham. *A Sort of Life.* New York: Pocket Books, 1973. Pp. 51-52, 80-82, 114-115, 149-150.

Hegner, William. *The Drum Beaters.* New York: Pocket Books, 1972. Pp. 16-17, 42-44, 102-104, 139-140.

Higgins, George. *The Friends of Eddie Coyle.* New York: Bantam Books, Inc. 1973. Pp. 58-60, 124-126, 148-150, 184-186.

Hodge, Jane Aiken. *Only a Novel.* Greenwich, Conn.: Fawcett Publications, Inc., 1973. Pp. 94-96, 143-144, 199-200, 244-245.

Holmes, Marjorie. *I've Got to Talk to Somebody, God.* New York: Bantam Books, Inc., 1971. Pp. xiii-xv, 36-38, 73-75, 111-113.

Holt, Victoria. *On the Night of the Seventh Moon.* Greenwich, Conn.: Fawcett Publications, Inc., 1972. Pp. 81-82, 160-162, 201-203, 272-273.

Houston, James. *The White Dawn.* New York: New American Library, 1972. Pp. 56-57, 111-112, 167-168, 214-215.

Houston, Penelope. *The Contemporary Cinema.* Baltimore: Penguin Books, Inc., 1963. Pp. 25-26, 68-69, 121-122, 142-143.

Howar, Barbara. *Laughing All the Way.* Greenwich, Conn.: Fawcett Publications, Inc., 1974. Pp. 33-34, 69-70, 121-122, 137-138.

Jaffe, Rona. *The Other Woman.* New York: Bantam Books, Inc., 1973. Pp. 44-45, 74-75, 148-150, 198-200.

Kazan, Elia. *The Assassins.* Greenwich, Conn.: Fawcett Publications, Inc., 1973. Pp. 84-86, 167-168, 230-232, 336-337.

Kemelman, Harry. *Saturday the Rabbi Went Hungry.* Greenwich, Conn.: Fawcett Publications, Inc., 1966. Pp. 18-19, 38-39, 67-68, 149-150.

Langer, Walter. *The Mind of Adolf Hitler.* New York: New American Library, 1973. Pp. 57-58, 88-89, 147-148, 206-207.

Lash, Joseph. *Eleanor and Franklin.* New York: New American Library, 1973. Pp. 253-254, 381-382, 601-602, 800-801.

LeShan, Eda. *Sex and Your Teen-Ager.* New York: Warner Books, Inc., 1973. Pp. 25-26, 70-71, 121-122, 180-181.

Levey, Jim. *Partings.* New York: Pyramid Books, 1974. Pp. 11-12, 73-74, 156-158, 220-222.

Lindbergh, Ann Morrow. *Hour of Gold, Hour of Lead.* New York: New American Library, 1974. Pp. 40-41, 87-89, 180-181, 262-264.

Longstreet, Stephen. *The Pedlock Inheritance.* New York: Pyramid Books, 1974. Pp. 106-107, 167-168, 287-288, 374-375.

Maas, Peter. *Serpico.* New York: Bantam Books, 1974. Pp. 74-75, 122-123, 203-204, 235-236.

MacDonald, Ross. *Sleeping Beauty.* New York: Bantam Books, Inc., 1974. Pp. 53-54, 79-81, 148-149, 212-214.

MacDougall, Ruth Doan. *The Cheerleader.* New York: Bantam Books, Inc., 1974. Pp. 42-43, 73-74, 146-148, 216-217.

Mailer, Norman. *Of a Fire on the Moon.* New York: New American Library, 1971. Pp. 48-49, 160-161, 247-248, 303-304.

Malamud, Bernard. *Rembrandt's Hat.* New York: Pocket Books, 1974. Pp. 70-72, 101-102, 134-135, 161-162.

Mander, John. *The Unrevolutionary Society.* New York: Harper & Row Publishers, Inc., 1971. Pp. 55-57, 124-125, 200-201, 273-274.

Mankiewicz, Frank. *Perfectly Clear.* New York: Popular Library, 1973. Pp. 87-88, 128-129, 179-180, 191-192.

Maynard, Joyce. *Looking Back.* New York: Avon Books, 1974. Pp. 31-32, 56-57, 90-91, 128-129.

Meacock, Norma. *Thinking Girl.* New York: Avon Books, 1974. Pp. 32-33, 68-69, 127-129, 183-184.

Millett, Kate. *Sexual Politics.* New York: Avon Books, 1971. Pp. 21-22, 89-90, 220-221, 331-332.

Mitford, Nancy. *Pigeon Pie.* New York: Curtis Books, 1951. Pp. 23-25, 61-62, 120-122, 146-148.

Montgomery, Ruth. *Here and Hereafter.* Greenwich, Conn.: Fawcett Publications, 1968. Pp. 24-25, 64-65, 105-106, 134-136.

Morgan, Elaine. *The Descent of Woman.* New York: Bantam Books, 1973. Pp. 66-68, 87-88, 163-164, 192-193.

Newman, Andrea. *The City Lover.* New York: Ballantine Books, 1971. Pp. 18-21, 43-44, 86-87, 104-105.

Oakley, Mary Ann B. *Elizabeth Cady Stanton.* Old Westbury, N.Y.: The Feminist Press, 1972. Pp. 27-29, 76-77, 96-98, 131-133.

Oates, Joyce Carol. *Them.* Greenwich, Conn.: Fawcett Publications, Inc., 1970. Pp. 126-127, 181-182, 281-282, 366-367.

O'Hara, John. *Hope of Heaven.* New York: Popular Library, 1938. Pp. 26-28, 58-59, 98-99, 122-123.

Peter, Lawrence J. *The Peter Prescription.* New York: Bantam Books, 1973. Pp. 53-56, 86-88, 140-142, 198-200.

Pilat, Oliver. *Drew Pearson.* New York: Pocket Books, 1973. Pp. 103-105, 118-119, 230-231, 287-288.

Plimpton, George. *Hank Aaron: One for the Record.* New York: Bantam Books, Inc., 1974. Pp. 11-12, 35-36, 60-61, 109-110.

Renault, Mary. *The Persian Boy.* New York: Bantam Books, 1974. Pp. 119-120, 212-213, 261-262, 337-338.

Rhys, Jean. *Good Morning, Midnight.* New York: Random House, Inc., 1974. Pp. 31-33, 71-72, 130-132, 156-158.

Rosten, Norman. *Marilyn.* New York: New American Library, 1973. Pp. 26-28, 42-44, 65-67, 79-81.

Roth, Philip. *The Great American Novel.* New York: Bantam Books, Inc., 1974. Pp. 107-108, 173-174, 251-252, 328-329.

Rovere, Richard. *The American Establishment.* New York: Harcourt, Brace & World, Inc., 1962. Pp. 68-69, 122-123, 158-159, 250-251.

Sakol, Jeannie. *I Was Never the Princess.* New York: Popular Library, 1971. Pp. 35-37, 56-58, 60-61, 129-130.

Salisbury, Harrison. *To Peking—And Beyond.* New York: Berkley Publishing Co., 1973. Pp. 55-56, 136-137, 272-273, 304-305.

Sanders, Marion K. *Dorothy Thompson.* New York: Avon Books, 1974. Pp. 85-86, 113-114, 163-164, 277-278.

Schreiber, Flora. *Sybil.* New York: Warner Books, Inc., 1974. Pp. 144-145, 224, 241, 281-282, 341-342.

Sheed, Wilfred. *People Will Always Be Kind.* New York: Dell Publishing Co., Inc., 1973. Pp. 9-10, 76-77, 123-124, 157-158.

Shulman, Alix Kates. *Memoirs of an Ex-Prom Queen.* New York: Bantam Books, Inc., 1974. Pp. 3-4, 50-51, 127-129, 222-224.

Simmons, Charles. *An Old-Fashioned Darling.* New York: New American Library, 1973. Pp. 35-36, 58-59, 86-87, 107-108.

Smith, Frank E. *The Politics of Conservation.* New York: Harper & Row Publishers, Inc., 1971. Pp. 31-32, 113-114, 160-162, 255-257.

Smith, Wilbur. *Gold Mine.* New York: Pyramid Books, 1973. Pp. 57-59, 76-78, 138-140, 221-223.

Steiner, Nancy. *A Closer Look at Ariel.* New York: Popular Library, 1973. Pp. 47-49, 64-66, 82-84, 102-104.

Stewart, Fred Mustard. *Lady Darlington.* New York: Bantam Books, Inc., 1973. Pp. 65-66, 115-116, 147-148, 235-236.

Stubbs, Jean. *Dear Laura.* Greenwich, Conn.: Fawcett Publications, Inc., 1973. Pp. 26-27, 48-49, 114-116, 165-167.

Taylor, Telford. *Nuremburg and Vietnam.* Chicago: Quadrangle Books, 1970. Pp. 39-41, 80-82, 127-129, 167-169.

Thompson, Ann Lorraine. *A Cry for Love.* New York: Avon Books, 1974. Pp. 49-50, 89-90, 170-172, 206-207.

Thompson, Hunter. *Fear and Loathing on the Campaign Trail '72.* New York: Popular Library, 1973. Pp. 100-101, 185-186, 259-260, 378-380.

Toffler, Alvin. *Future Shock.* New York: Bantam Books, Inc., 1971. Pp. 193-195, 229-230, 371-373, 429-430.

Uhnak, Dorothy. *Law and Order.* New York: Pocket Books, 1974. Pp. 10-11, 122-123, 189-190, 336-337.

Vilar, Esther. *The Manipulated Man.* New York: Bantam Books, Inc., 1974. Pp. 17-18, 55-56, 82-84, 113-114.

Vonnegut, Kurt. *Slaughterhouse Five.* New York: Dell Publishing Co., Inc., 1971. Pp. 41-43, 62-64, 113-115, 159-161.

Wallace, Irving. *The Seven Minutes.* New York: Pocket Books, 1970. Pp. 157-158, 287-288, 390-391, 522-524.

Wicker, Tom. *Facing the Lions.* New York: Avon Books, 1974. Pp. 138-139, 200-201, 296-297, 345-346.